POCKET

DUBROVNIK & THE DALMATIAN COAST

TOP SIGHTS · LOCAL EXPERIENCES

Date: 7/12/19

914.972 DUB 2019
Dragicevich, Peter,
Dubrovnik & the Dalmatian
Coast : tip sights, local

PALM BEACH COUNTY
LIBRARY SYSTEM
3650 SUMMIT BLVD.
WEST PALM BEACH, FL 33406

PETER DRAGICEVICH

Contents

Plan Your Trip

Trogir (p154)
JOHN AND TINA REID/GETTY IMAGES ©

Explore Dubrovnik & the Dalmatian Coast

Worth a Trip

Survival Guide

Special Features

Welcome to Dubrovnik & the Dalmatian Coast

If your Mediterranean fantasies feature balmy days by sapphire waters in the shade of ancient walled towns, Dalmatia is the place to turn them into reality. The extraordinary island-speckled coastline is backed by rugged mountains and bookended by two of Croatia's most intriguing cities: Dubrovnik, to the south, and Split, to the north.

Dubrovnik (p33)
S.F/SHUTTERSTOCK ©

Top Sights

Dubrovnik City Walls & Forts

The world's finest city walls. **p34**

Diocletian's Palace

A vibrant, living, ancient quarter. **p124**

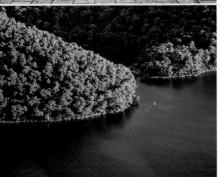

Mljet National Park

Forest, lakes and ancient ruins. **p86**

Trogir

World Heritage walled city. **p154**

Ston Walls

Dramatic peninsula-spanning fortifications. **p72**

St Mark's Cathedral

A masterwork in stone. **p92**

DANITA DELIMONT/GETTY IMAGES ©

LUMI IMAGES/ROMULIC-STOCIC/GETTY IMAGES ©

Pakleni Islands

Hvar Town's offshore playground. **p102**

Lokrum Island

Dubrovnik's idyllic island escape. **p66**

Klis Fortress

Mountain stronghold offering outstanding outlook. **p152**

Srđ

Unsurpassed old-town views. **p40**

SAMANTHA OHLSEN/ALAMY STOCK PHOTO ©

DREAMER4787/SHUTTERSTOCK ©

Salona

Roaming a Roman city. **p148**

Zlatni Rat

The supermodel of Croatia's beaches. **p114**

Eating

Croatian food echoes the cultures that have influenced it over its history. In Dalmatia the primary influence is Venice and the cuisine is typically Mediterranean. Favourite ingredients include olive oil, garlic, flat-leaf parsley, bay leaves and all manner of seafood. Meals often begin with a first course of pasta or rižoto (risotto).

PAUL PRESCOTT/SHUTTERSTOCK ©

Specialties

For a special appetiser, try *paški sir*, a pungent hard sheep's cheese from the island of Pag. Lamb from Pag is deemed Croatia's best; they feed on wild herbs, which gives the meat a distinct flavour. It's traditionally enjoyed either spit-roasted or cooked *ispod peka* (roasted under a metal dome topped with hot coals; pictured above right). At restaurants, *peka* dishes usually need to be ordered in advance.

Seafood favourites include baked whole fish, fried *lignje* (squid, sometimes stuffed with cheese and prosciutto) and *hobotnica* (octopus, either carpaccio, in a salad or cooked under a *peka*).

Other regional specialties include *brodet* (a seafood stew served with polenta; also known as *brodetto*, *brudet* or *brujet*, depending on which part of the coast you're from) and *pašticada* (beef stewed in wine, prunes and spices and served with gnocchi). The most typical side dish is *blitva* (Swiss chard served with slightly mushy potatoes and drenched in olive oil and garlic).

Best Dalmatian

Konoba Marjan This unassuming Split tavern is one of the best places for traditional seafood in Dalmatia. (p139)

Kapetanova Kuća Feast on Ston oysters, metres from the waters from which they're harvested. (p73)

Vinotoka Try lamb or octopus *ispod peka*, or a delicious seafood pasta in this informal Supetar tavern. (p118)

Konoba Fetivi Seafood specialities in the backstreets of Split. (p139)

Pojoda This Vis Town restaurant serves interesting seafood stews. (p142)

JURE/GETTY IMAGES ©

Konoba Matejuška One of a trio of excellent seafood taverns in the Veli Varoš neighbourhood of Split. (p139; pictured above left)

Best Fine Dining

Restaurant 360° Dubrovnik's finest offers contemporary dining perched right on the famous city walls. (p53)

Nautika Elegant fine dining overlooking Dubrovnik's old town. (p53)

Zoi This upmarket Split restaurant delivers modern Mediterranean cuisine in glitzy surrounds. (p139)

Proto Serving seafood delicacies to Dubrovnik visitors since the late 19th century. (p54)

Restaurant Dubrovnik Snazzy rooftop-terrace restaurant hidden down a back lane. (p54)

Best Modern Mediterranean

Bugenvila Gorgeously presented, adventurous cuisine on the Cavtat waterfront. (p56)

Pantarul Zesty Mediterranean cooking in Dubrovnik's Lapad neighbourhood. (p69)

Best Vegetarian

Nishta Strictly vegan, and one of old-town Dubrovnik's best eateries. (p51)

Makrovega Unassuming vegetarian restaurant on a Split backstreet. (p138)

Best Italian

Portofino Upmarket Italian on a square at the very centre of Diocletian's Palace in Split. (p140)

Aterina Seafood features prominently at this Korčula Town restaurant. (p98)

La Casa Delicious pizza, pasta, risotto and grills in Orebić. (p78)

Best Japanese

Shizuku Japanese owners ensure authenticity at this elegant restaurant in the backstreets of Lapad, Dubrovnik. (p69)

Bota Šare Oyster & Sushi Bar Delicious sushi tucked away in a lane facing Dubrovnik's cathedral. (p53)

Wine

CANVASPIX/SHUTTERSTOCK ©

Wine from Croatia may be a novelty to international consumers but vino has been an embedded part of the region's lifestyle for more than 25 centuries. Today the tradition is undergoing a renaissance in the hands of a new generation of winemakers with a focus on preserving indigenous varietals and revitalising ancestral estates.

Dalmatian Varietals

Dalmatia, with its island vineyards, fosters a fascinating array of indigenous grape varieties that prosper in the Mediterranean climate, yielding full-bodied wines of rich character. Here *plavac mali*, scion of zinfandel (*crljenik kašteljanski*) and the obscure *dobričić,* is king of reds. Wines labelled 'Dingač' are *plavac mali* from a specific mountainside high above the sea on the Pelješac Peninsula that's widely regarded as producing Croatia's best reds (see p76). Production is tiny and good examples command premium prices.

Other indigenous varieties worth seeking are *babić* (red), *pošip* (an elegant white, the best of which is from the island of Korčula), *grk* (a fruit-driven white, exclusively produced in Lumbarda on Korčula) and *malvasija* (a white from the Kvarner region, near Dubrovnik, not to be confused with *malvazija* with a 'z' from Istria). For easy-chair quaffing, the lovely rosés of Dalmatia are perfect for lazy Mediterranean days.

Most Croatian wineries are family-owned estates and not all have visitor-ready facilities; appointments are recommended.

Best Wineries

Stina Right on the waterfront in Bol, this Brač winery has an impressive tasting room in a historic wine-collective warehouse. (p117)

Grgić Vina Californian wine-making legend Mike Grgich's family vineyard, producing top-flight *plavac mali* and *pošip*. (p76)

STJEPAN TAFRA/SHUTTERSTOCK ©

Matuško Wines Try *plavac mali* at its best, from the Dingač appellation. (p76)

Korta Katarina Orebić winery offering a variety of wine and food tastings. (p77)

Vina Carić A combination cellar door and wine bar in Vrboska on the island of Hvar. (p110)

Best Wine Bars

Paradox Upmarket Split wine bar, with an extraordinary selection. (p141)

D'vino The best spot in Dubrovnik to sample a wide range of Croatian wines. (p54)

Malvasija Relaxed and friendly Dubrovnik wine bar, with tasty snack platters. (p57)

3 Pršuta Sophisticated wine and nibbles in Hvar's walled town. (p111)

Vinum Bonum Chilled-out drinks in Korčula's back streets. (p98)

Grabovac Makarska showcase for an Imotski winemaker. (p82)

Taverna Domanoeta Rustic tavern on the Pelješac Peninsula offering homemade wine and food. (p76)

Best Wine Shops

Peninsula A combination wine shop and bar, showcasing wines from the Pelješac Peninsula. (p76)

Vina Miličić Dubrovnik store selling wine from the Miličić winery, along with other producers. (p65)

Kawa Funky Dubrovnik design store which also stocks local wines and craft beers. (p43)

Wine Regions

Croatia is roughly divided into four winemaking regions (Slavonia, Croatian Uplands, Istria and Dalmatia) with 16 distinct subregions *(vinogorje)* recognised as Protected Designations of Origin.

Drinking & Nightlife

Cafe-bars are ubiquitous throughout Dalmatia – they're places where locals go to shoot the breeze for hours at a time. The liveliest bar scenes can be found in Split and, in summer, Hvar. You won't go thirsty in Dubrovnik either – the city has Irish pubs, cliff-edge bars, wine bars and lots of cafe-bars. And that's just the old town.

Local Tipples

Croatia is famous for its *rakija* (potent fruit brandy), which comes in different flavours. The most commonly drunk are *loza* (made from grapes, like the Italian grappa), *šljivovica* (from plums) and *travarica* (from herbs). The island of Vis is famous for its delicious *rogačica* (from carob). It's customary to have a small glass of *rakija* before a meal. Other popular drinks include *vinjak* (cognac), mara-schino (cherry liqueur made in Zadar), *prošek* (sweet dessert wine) and *pelinkovac* (herbal liqueur).

The two most popular types of Croatian *pivo* (beer) are Zagreb's Ožujsko and Karlovačko from Karlovac.

Strongly brewed *kava* (espresso-style coffee), served in tiny cups, is popular throughout Croatia. You can have it diluted with milk (macchiato) or order a cappuccino. Although some places have decaf options this is considered somewhat sacrile-gious, as Croats love their coffee. When locals talk of tea (*čaj*), they're usually referring to the herbal kind; black tea can be hard to find. Tap water is drinkable.

Best Beach Bars

Hula-Hula Hvar The ultimate trashy-glam beach bar. (p111)

Bard Mala Buža Cocktails on the cliff – a consummate Dubrovnik experience. (p54)

Buža Dubrovnik's most popular clifftop bar. (p55)

Cave Bar More Sit in the sun by the water or cool off within the cave itself. (p69)

Coral Beach Club Du-brovnik's glitziest beach bar. (p69)

Carpe Diem Beach Rau-cous bar in the Pakleni

Islands, off Hvar Town, famous for its all-night parties. (p103)

Best Bohemian Cafe-Bars

Marcvs Marvlvs Spalatensis Atmospheric library-styled wine bar hidden within Diocletian's Palace. (p140)

Art Cafe Dubrovnik's hippest bar is a great spot for a smoothie, a coffee or something stronger. (p58)

Academia Ghetto Club Split's artsy crowd gravitates to this eclectic old-town bar. (p143)

Rock Caffe Exit Hard-rocking live-music bar, within Dubrovnik's old town. (p57)

Best Craft-beer Bars

Beer Garden Sample local brews and dude food in the courtyard of this Supetar pub. (p118)

Dubrovnik Beer Factory Old-town refuge for craft-beer aficionados. (p55)

Glam Beer Therapy Another good spot to sample local brews in Dubrovnik's old town. (p59)

Best Cocktail Bars

Carpe Diem Hvar Town's swankiest cocktail joint, with a large see-and-be-seen terrace. (p111)

Varadero Buzzy Bol cocktail terrace with a tropical vibe. (p121)

Best Dance Bars

Kiva Bar The party quickly packs out this tiny bar and takes over the lane. (p111)

St Riva Cocktails and trashy fun within the seafront wall of Diocletian's Palace, Split. (p143)

Best Clubs

Revelin Dubrovnik's renowned nightclub, within the old-town fortifications. (p57)

Zenta Split's best club, right by the water. (p131)

Deep A summertime Makarska club in the depths of a sea cave. (p82)

For Kids

With safe beaches and lots of ancient towns and fortresses for would-be knights and princesses to explore, Dalmatia offers entertainment aplenty for those with children in tow. Wander the maze that is Diocletian's Palace, head to the beaches, and let the little ones off the leash in the car-free old towns of Dubrovnik and Korčula.

Things To Do

Dalmatia has a lot of open spaces, playgrounds aplenty and pedestrian zones where there's no danger of traffic. Most seaside towns have a *riva* (seafront promenade) away from the water's edge that's perfect for strolling and letting the toddlers run around.

There are beaches galore, although some of what are referred to as 'beaches' are rocky indentations with steep drop-offs. Many of the sandy beaches are extremely shallow: perfect for toddlers but not so great for the teens. The numerous pebbly beaches tend to offer better swimming.

Keep in mind that some of the smaller seaside towns can be too quiet for fun-seeking teenagers. They (and you in turn) will be a lot happier in the more happening coastal destinations where there are buzzy cafes and seasonal funfair rides.

Children's discounts are widely available for everything from museum admissions to hotel accommodation. The cut-off age is often nine, when student discounts kick in. Many attractions offer free entry for the little ones.

Best Eating

Restoran Perlica Aside from being the go-to place for spit-roasted meat in the vicinity of Split, Perlica has an excellent, well-equipped playground. (p153)

Konoba Maslina This family-friendly tavern on the island of Korčula has a little playground to keep the tots occupied while you wait for your meals. (p98)

Best Beaches

Lapad Bay A favourite with Dubrovnik families due to its gentle waters, floating

DARIOS/SHUTTERSTOCK ©

playground, land-based playground and a long pedestrian promenade lined with snack bars and ice-cream parlours. (p69)

Makarska Town Beach Kids love tearing around this long beach and its associated promenade. There's lots to do, including an inflatable playground and summertime fun park. (p81)

Prapratno A great family option as it's sandy enough for sandcastles and deep enough for the older kids, while still being very calm and safe. (p73)

Pržina Another excellent sandy beach, near Lumbarda on the island of Korčula. (p17)

Mljet National Park Malo Jezero, the smaller of the saltwater lakes, is warm and perfect for swimming with little ones. (p87)

Copacabana Beach This pebbly Dubrovnik beach has a floating playground and kayaks for hire. (p69)

Bačvice There's always plenty to see and do at Split's most popular beach, and loads of places for a snack afterwards. (p131)

Best Entertainment

Split City Puppet Theatre Great for the little kids, even if much of the action is in Croatian. (p145)

Moreška Cultural Club Check out Korčula's colourful sword dance: a stylised battle between two kings fighting over a princess. (p99)

Sea Urchins

Be mindful of the numerous sea urchins in the shallows, particularly on rocky beaches; invest in some plastic water shoes for safer playing.

Shopping

You'll find malls and chain stores in Split, but the best souvenirs are the local specialties, such as lavender and lace from Hvar, and stoneware from Brač. Croatian embroidery is distinguished by cheerful red geometric patterns set against a white background, which you'll see on tablecloths, pillowcases and blouses.

GAMEOVER2012/GETTY IMAGES ©

Dubrovnik Shopping

Dubrovnik is far from a shopper's paradise. Stradun is mostly lined with tacky souvenir shops, although there are a handful of more interesting stores hidden down the side lanes.

Hvar Shopping

Lavender, lavender and more lavender is sold in bottles, flasks, sachets and little fragrant bags. Depending on the time of year, there will be anywhere from one to 50 stalls along Hvar Town's harbour selling the substance, its aroma saturating the air. Various herbal oils, potions, skin creams and salves are also hawked.

Split Shopping

Central Split is filled with stores catering to the tourist market and cashed-up locals. Marmontova is the main shopping strip, with the biggest names, but you'll find some interesting local boutiques scattered around Diocletian's Palace.

Best Bookshops

Kutak Knjiga An excellent little multilingual bookstore in Korčula. (p99)

Algebra Dubrovnik bookseller, with a range of Croatian classics in English. (p63)

Best Craft & Design

Kawa Hip locally designed jewellery, T-shirts and gifts, in Dubrovnik. (p43)

Studio Naranča Original art, T-shirts and tote bags, in Split. (p146)

Medusa Dubrovnik store selling locally made soaps, craft and chocolates. (p61)

NINO MARCUTTI/ALAMY STOCK PHOTO ©

Best Fashion & Accessories

Arterija Homegrown women's fashion and jewellery in Split's old town. (p145)

Bag & Co Interesting handbags and tote bags, also in old-town Split. (p145)

Think Pink Split store selling Croatian-designed women's clothing and jewellery. (p146)

Best Food

Uje Purveyors of fine Dalmatian olive oil, jams, honey, chocolate and wine, with branches in Dubrovnik and Split. (p61)

Terra Croatica Dubrovnik Everything's Croatian made, including olive oil, wine, chocolates and craft. (p59)

Bonbonnière Kraš Croatia's most famous chocolatier has branches in Dubrovnik and Split. (p63)

Best Markets

Diocletian's Cellars Good-quality souvenirs in the basement of the Split palace. (p146)

Fish Market An age-old slice of Split life. (p146)

Small Loggia Stalls sell jewellery in this historic covered market in Trogir. (p157)

Grad Market Craft stalls in old-town Dubrovnik. (p63)

Green Market The best place in Split to stock up on fresh local produce. (p147)

Croatian Lace

Croatia's finest artisan product is the intricate lace from the islands of Pag and Hvar, part of a centuries-old tradition that is still going strong.

Beaches

Dalmatia is blessed with one of the most unrelentingly gorgeous stretches of coast on the Mediterranean, with crystalline waters and a backdrop that changes from mountains to walled towns to low-slung islands and back again. In summer the water temperature can reach over 25°C, and it's usually over 20°C from June to October.

Swimming

If you're expecting long sandy beaches to compete with Bondi, Malibu or Copacabana, you'll be disappointed. Mostly you'll find pretty little rocky or pebbly coves, edged by pines, olive trees or low scrub. There are some sandy beaches – mainly on the islands.

What is particularly striking all the way along the coast is the clarity and colour of the water, at times seeming almost unnaturally blue or green. The European Environment Agency rates 98% of Croatia's bathing sites as having excellent water quality.

Swimmers should watch out for sea urchins, which are common along the coast. The sharp spines are painful to tread on and can break off in your skin and become infected.

Croatia is not short of places to let it all hang out, with naturist beaches all along the coast. Look for the signs reading 'FKK', which stands for *freikörperkultur,* meaning 'free body culture' in German.

Best Dubrovnik Beaches

Sveti Jakov Beach Clear waters, a beach cafe and views back towards the old town. (p43)

Bellevue Beach Surrounding cliffs, afternoon shade and cliff divers to ogle. (p48)

Best Split Beaches

Kašjuni The least urban of Split's beaches, with the green crest of Marjan Forest Park as a backdrop. (p133)

Bačvice Great people-watching and a constant buzz, but extraordinarily busy. (p131)

KITE_RIN/SHUTTERSTOCK ©

Best Sandy Beaches

Prapratno One of the mainland's rare sandy beaches, tucked away on the Pelješac Peninsula. (p73)

Pržina A family favourite near Lumbarda on the island of Korčula. (p21)

Best Pebbly Beaches

Zlatni Rat A protrusion of pebbles packed with beach bodies, bars and activities galore. (p114)

Pasjača Close to Dubrovnik but off the beaten track, this Konavle beach is a hidden delight. (p60)

Punta Rata The best of Brela's string of pine-fringed pebble coves. (p82)

Best for Naturists

Nugal Near Makarska, this is the prettiest of Dalmatia's nude beaches. (p82; pictured)

Jerolim The closest of the Pakleni Islands to Hvar Town is completely clothing optional. (p103)

Sea Conditions

In summer, the Adriatic can more closely resemble a millpond than the sea, but the waves pick up when the wild wind known as the *bora* arrives in winter.

Boat Cruises & Rental

MOUNTAINPIX/SHUTTERSTOCK ©

Sail Croatia (www.sail-croatia.com) Offers a booze-fuelled week-long cruise from Split to Dubrovnik aimed at twenty-somethings – as well as a range of options for a more mature crowd.

Dubrovnik Boats (☑098 757 890; www.dubrovnikboats.com; ACI Marina Dubrovnik, Na Skali 2, Komolac) Private speedboat tours to the Elafiti Islands, Mljet and Korčula.

Dubrovnik Boat Rentals (☑095 90 45 799; www.dubrovnik boatrentals.com; Anice Bošković 6, Pile) Half- or full-day private speedboat trips to Lokrum, Cavtat, the Elafiti Islands, Mljet and Korčula.

Nautic Center Bol (☑098 361 651; www.nautic-center-bol.com; Zlatnog rata 9a; ☉Jun-Oct) Rents boats and offers cruises to Hvar and Korčula.

Alter Natura (☑021-717 239; www.alternatura.hr; Hrvatskih mučenika 2) Based in Komiža on Vis Island, this adventure-tour specialist offers boat trips to caves and hard-to-get-to beaches.

Summer Blues (☑021-332 501; www.summer-blues.com; Tončićeva 4; half/full day from €58/65; ☉May-Oct) Sailing trips from Split to Bol (€87) or Hvar and the Pakleni Islands (€92) on board a luxurious cat-amaran, with dance music, cocktails and lunch included.

Šugaman Tours (☑021-344 085; www.sugamantours.com; Dosud 4; ☉8am-10pm Apr-Oct, to noon Mon-Fri Nov-Mar) Speedboat trips from Split to the 'Blue Lagoon' and Trogir (€60), or to Hvar and the Blue Cave (€125).

Hvar Pub Crawl (☑097 68 03 717; www.hvarpubcrawl.com; Obala Riva; crawl €25-35; ☉May-Sep) This all-night booze cruise starts at 10.30pm with an hour-long trip around the Pakleni Islands, followed by bars and a club.

Walking Tours

UYGARGEOGRAPHIC/GETTY IMAGES ©

Dubrovnik Walks
(📞 095 80 64 526; www.
dubrovnikwalks.com;
Brsalje 8, Pile; 🕐 Mar-
Dec) Excellent English-
language guided
walks departing from
near the Pile Gate,
including 90-minute
old-town (120KN)
and *Game of Thrones*
(150KN) tours, and
a two-hour 'Walls &
Wars' tour (130KN);
no reservations
necessary between
April and October.
They also offer 2½-
hour sea-kayaking
tours (day/sunset
230/250KN).

Dubrovnik Day Tours
(📞 098 17 51 775; www.
dubrovnikdaytours.net)
Sightseeing and *Game
of Thrones* tours
around Dubrovnik,

as well as private day
trips led by licensed
guides to as far away
as Korčula, Split,
Kotor, Budva, Mostar
and Sarajevo. They
also offer tailored
small-group tours tar-
geted to cruise-ship
passengers, and mar-
keted as Dubrovnik
Shore Tours (www.
dubrovnikshoretours.
net).

Split Walking Tours
(📞 099 82 15 383; www.
splitwalkingtour.com;
Dioklecijanova 3) Leads
walking tours in Eng-
lish, Spanish, Italian,
German and French,
departing from the
Golden Gate at set
times during the day
(check the website).
Options include the
75-minute Diocle-

tian's Palace Tour
(100KN) and the two-
hour Split Walking
Tour (160KN), which
includes the palace
and the medieval part
of town. It also offers
kayaking, diving, cy-
cling tours, boat trips
and excursions.

Ziggy Star (📞 099 54
97 385; www.pubcrawl
split.net; crawl €15;
🕐 from 10pm) Named,
presumably, after the
mythical rocker who
took it all too far, Ziggy
Star offers an opportu-
nity to push your limits
in a guided all-night
bender in Split. Start-
ing with a 'power hour'
of cocktails and shoot-
ers, the trail leads to a
bar on the Riva, then a
club, then breakfast.

Four Perfect Days

Day 1

EMICRISTEA/GETTY IMAGES ©

Spend the morning exploring Dubrovnik's extraordinary old town. Start early and take a walk along the **city walls** (p34) before it gets too hot. Spend the rest of the morning wandering the marbled streets and calling into whichever church, palace or museum takes your fancy.

After lunch, take the cable car up **Srđ** (p40), stopping at the top to visit the exhibition **Dubrovnik During the Homeland War** (p41). Afterwards, head down to **Banje Beach** (p43) for a dip.

Start your evening with sunset drinks at **Buža** (p55), then splurge on a romantic meal at **Restaurant 360°** (p53), before sampling fine Croatian wines at **D'vino** (p54).

Day 2

Head up the coast, stopping to check out the **Trsteno Arboretum** (p75; pictured) and the **Ston Walls** (p72) before sitting down for a seafood lunch at **Kapetanova Kuća** (p73) in Mali Ston.

Continue along the Pelješac Peninsula, potentially stopping at **Prapratno** (p73) for a swim, and at a winery along the way. Take a quick look around Orebić before boarding the ferry to Korčula Town.

Check into your accommodation then take a stroll around the old town, paying a visit to **St Mark's Cathedral** (p92). Head to **Massimo** (p99) atop the Zakerjan Tower for a sunset cocktail, then to dinner at **LD Terrace** (p97) on the waterfront promenade.

Day 3

DREAMER4787/GETTY IMAGES ©

Catch an early-morning catamaran to Hvar Town. After you've dropped your bags take a wander around the centre of town, calling into the **Franciscan Monastery** (p106) and **St Stephen's Cathedral** (p105) before heading to lunch at one of the many excellent eateries.

After lunch, take a leisurely taxi-boat ride to the **Pakleni Islands** (p102; pictured) and spend the rest of the afternoon swimming and relaxing. Aim to be back on the mainland well before sunset so that you can freshen up before hitting **Hula-Hula Hvar** (p111).

Once the post-beach party starts to wind down, make your way back into the centre of town for a meal. Afterwards, rejoin the party at **Kiva Bar** (p111).

Day 4

Catch an early boat to Split and spend most of your day immersed in the surreal workaday ancient world of **Diocletian's Palace** (p124). Visit the peristil, the cathedral and the Temple of Jupiter, head down to check out the substructure, and then wander through the **vestibule** (p127; pictured) and call into the **Ethnographic Museum** (p137) and **City Museum** (p136).

Stop to rub the big toe of the **Grgur Ninski statue** (p136) and then walk up to **Marjan Forest Park** (p133) for a leafy stroll. Stay to watch the sunset views from **Vidilica** (p133).

Make your way back down the hill and stop at one of the superb local seafood restaurants in Vela Varoš before hitting the bars on the **Riva** (p136).

Need to Know

For detailed information, see Survival Guide p159

Language
Croatian

Currency
Kuna (KN)

Visas
Generally not required for stays of up to 90 days. Some nationalities (such as Chinese, Indian, Russian, South African and Turkish) do need them.

Money
ATMs are widely available. Credit cards are accepted in most hotels and restaurants. Smaller restaurants, shops and private-accommodation owners only take cash.

Mobile Phones
Users with unlocked phones can buy a local SIM card; they're easy to find. Otherwise, you may be charged roaming rates.

Time
Central European Time (GMT/UTC plus one hour)

Daily Budget

Budget: Less than 600KN
Dorm bed: 100–360KN

Pizza or pasta: 40–70KN

Short bus journey: 11–15KN

Midrange: 600–1400KN
Double room in a hotel: 450–900KN

Meal in a decent restaurant: 70-200KN

Admission to museums: 20–42KN

Top end: More than 1400KN
Double room in a luxury hotel: from 900KN

Meal in a top restaurant: 150–900KN

Private sailing trip: 1000KN

Car rental per day: 450KN

Useful Websites

Chasing the Donkey (www.chasingthedonkey.com) Entertaining travel blog by an Aussie family of Croatian extraction living in Dalmatia.

Croatian Tourism (www.croatia.hr) Official tourism site; the best start for holiday planning.

Croatia Times (www.croatia-times.com) Click on the Like Croatia tab for an information-packed online guide to Croatia.

Lonely Planet (www.lonelyplanet.com/croatia) Destination information, hotel bookings, traveller forum and more.

Parks of Croatia (www.parkovihrvatske.hr) Covers Croatia's national and nature parks.

Taste of Croatia (www.tasteofcroatia.org) Excellent and informative culinary website.

Arriving in Dalmatia

✈ Dubrovnik Airport

Atlas runs the airport bus service (40KN, 30 minutes), timed around flights. Buses to Dubrovnik stop at the Pile Gate and the bus station. A taxi costs up to 280KN.

✈ Split Airport

An airport shuttle bus heads to the main bus station at least 14 times a day (30KN, 30 minutes). Local buses 37 and 38 stop near the airport every 20 minutes, heading to Split (17KN) or Trogir (13KN). Taxis to Split cost between 250KN and 300KN.

✈ Brač Airport

There's no public transport, so you'll need to take a taxi (150KN to Bol, 300KN to Supetar) or collect a hire car.

Getting Around

✈ Air

Seasonal flights between Split and Dubrovnik.

⚓ Boat

Sizeable network of car ferries and faster catamarans between the coastal cities and the islands. Split is the main hub.

🚌 Bus

Reasonably priced, with regular services up and down the coastal highway. Island services are more limited but connect the major towns on Korčula, Hvar and Brač.

🚗 Car

Useful for travelling at your own pace, or for visiting regions with minimal public transport. Cars can be hired in every city or larger town. Drive on the right.

Dubrovnik & the Dalmatian Coast Regions

Trogir ⊙

Split Airport ✈

Klis Fortress ⊙ ⊙

Salona

Split (p123)
A lively, buzzy city that's both historic and modern.

Brač Airport ✈

Pakleni Islands ⊙

Hvar Town & Hvar Island (p101)
The sunniest spot in the country, with elegant restaurants and a buzzing nightlife.

Bol & Brač Island (p113)
Central Dalmatia's largest island has dramatic steep cliffs, inky waters and pine forests.

Dalmatian Coast (p71)

Historic towns and stunning beaches are strung along the coast, with a dramatic mountain backdrop.

BOSNIA & HERCEGOVINA

Korčula Town & Korčula Island (p91)

Historic coastal citadel surrounded by vineyards, olive groves and villages.

Ston Walls

Mljet National Park

Dubrovnik (p33)

A unique, betwitching city in a sublime setting; the essence of a medieval Mediterranean fantasy.

Lokrum Island

Dubrovnik Airport

Explore
Dubrovnik & the Dalmatian Coast

Worth a Trip 👀

Walking Tours 🥾

Hvar Town (p101) © SANTIAGO URQUIJO/GETTY IMAGES ©

Explore ⬡
Dubrovnik

Ringed by mighty defensive walls that dip their feet in the cerulean sea, Dubrovnik (population 28,500) encapsulates the very essence of a medieval Mediterranean fantasy. The city is simply unique; its beauty is bewitching, its setting sublime. Thousands of visitors walk along its marble streets every day, gazing, gasping and happily snapping away.

Start with a walk around the City Walls (p34) and then descend into the old town to explore its labyrinthine lanes and the grand spread of its main street, Placa. Take time to visit at least a few of its numerous churches, monasteries and museums, the top options being the Rector's Palace (p46), War Photo Limited (p46) and the fresco-covered St Ignatius of Loyola Church (p47). Climb up to the cable car and take a ride to the top of Srđ (p40). Finish your day with a stroll through Ploče and Viktorija (p42), ending with a dip at Sveti Jakov Beach (p43).

Getting There & Around

Dubrovnik's old town is compact and car-free.

✈ There's a major international airport at Čilipi, just south of Dubrovnik.

🚌 Coaches head to Dubrovnik from neighbouring countries and from all over Croatia.

⚓ From April to November, car ferries travel between Dubrovnik and Bari in Italy. Local ferries link Dubrovnik to various islands and to Split.

Dubrovnik Map on p44

Dubrovnik's Old Town CGE2010/SHUTTERSTOCK ©

Top Sights 📷
City Walls & Forts

Dubrovnik's defining feature is the imposing ring of walls that encircles its historic core. From the sea, the juxtaposition of pinkish-grey stone and azure waters is mesmerising, while from above the tight maze of church steeples and terracotta roofs is the setting for a fairy tale – or, at the very least, an HBO series featuring queens and dragons.

◉ MAP P44, F3

Gradske zidine

☎ 020-638 800

www.wallsofdubrovnik.
com

adult/child 150/50KN

🕙 8am-6.30pm Apr-Oct,
9am-3pm Nov-Mar

The Need for Walls

The natural protection afforded by its rocky cliffs first enticed refugees from the Roman town of Epidaurum (present-day Cavtat) to settle here in the 7th century.

The first set of walls to enclose the city was built in the 9th century and was strong enough to resist a 15-month siege by the Saracens. In the middle of the 14th century the 1.5m-thick defences were fortified with 15 square forts. The threat of attacks from the Turks in the 15th century prompted the city to strengthen the existing forts and add new ones, so that the entire old town was contained within a stone barrier 2km long and up to 25m high. The walls are thicker on the land side – up to 6m – and range from 1.5m to 3m on the sea side.

Round Fort Minčeta protects the landward edge of the city from attack, and Fort Bokar and Fort Lawrence look west and out to sea, while Fort Revelin and Fort St John guard the eastern approach and the Old Harbour.

The deep moat that once separated the city from the land is now filled with parks, car parks and a road.

City Gates

Historically, the entrance to the city was via two elaborate gates: the **Pile Gate** (Gradska vrata Pile) to the west and the **Ploče Gate** (Vrata od Ploča) to the east. Both have drawbridges that were raised at sunset when the doors were locked and the keys handed to the rector. A third entrance, the **Buža Gate**, was added to the northern wall at the top of Boškovićeva street in 1907.

The most impressive of the three is the Pile Gate, built in 1537, which remains the main entrance to the town. Note the stone **Statue of St Blaise**, holding the city in his hands, set in a niche over the Renaissance portal. This 4th-century Armenian martyr is Dubrovnik's patron

★ Top Tips

o The entrance to the walls nearest to the Pile Gate tends to be the busiest. Skip the queues by entering from the Ploče side, which has the added advantage of getting the steepest climbs out of the way first.

o Don't underestimate how strenuous the walk can be, especially on a hot day.

o There's very little shelter, so wear a hat and try to time your visit for the beginning or end of the day. You may avoid the worst of the crowds too.

o Take water with you; the vendors on the route tend to be overpriced.

✕ Take a Break

Cool off with an extra-creamy gelato from Dolce Vita (p50), the old town's best ice-cream parlour.

For a different perspective on the walls and a post-walk swim, cut through to Buža Bar (p55).

saint, and similar images are positioned in various parts of the wall and above all the major entrances. After passing through the outer gate you'll enter a large court with a ramp and stairs heading down to the inner gate, dating from 1460 and topped by a statue of St Blaise by leading Croatian sculptor Ivan Meštrović (1883–1962).

Wall Walk

There are ticketed entrances to the city walls near the Pile Gate, the Ploče Gate and the Maritime Museum. To reduce congestion, you're required to walk the walls in an anticlockwise direction. At busy times it can resemble a sweaty, slow-moving conga line. Don't let that put you off: the views over the old town and the shimmering Adriatic are worth any frustration resulting from a busy period.

One of the most charming aspects of the walk (although perhaps not for Dubrovnik's long-suffering residents) is the glimpses it gives into hidden gardens and courtyards in the residential fringes of the town.

Starting from the Ploče Gate entrance, you'll quickly reach **St Luke's Tower** (1467), facing the Old Harbour and Fort Revelin. The northern, landward section of wall is the highest, reaching a peak at rounded **Fort Minčeta** (Tvrđava Minčeta) at the city's northwestern corner. This massive structure was completed in 1464 to designs by Juraj Dalmatinac who is most famous as the creator of Šibenik's extraordinary cathedral. The battlements at the top provide remarkable views over the old town's rooftops.

Fort Lawrence (p38)

Dubrovnik: Destruction & Reconstruction

From late 1991 to May 1992, images of the shelling of Dubrovnik by the Yugoslav army dominated the news worldwide. For no obvious military or strategic reason, Dubrovnik was pummelled with some 2000 shells, causing considerable damage and loss of life. While memories may have faded for those who watched it from afar, those who suffered through it will never forget – and the city of Dubrovnik is determined that visitors should not either.

Shells struck 68% of the 824 buildings in the old town, leaving holes in two out of three tiled roofs. You can get a good impression of the extent of the damage while walking around the city walls: those roofs sporting bright new terracotta suffered damage and had to be replaced. The softer-toned original tiles are in a clear minority.

Building facades and the paving stones of streets and squares suffered 314 direct hits and there were 111 strikes on the wall itself. Nine historic palaces were completely gutted by fire, while the Sponza Palace, Rector's Palace, St Blaise's Church, Franciscan Monastery and the carved fountains Amerling and Onofrio all sustained serious damage. The reconstruction bill was estimated at US$10 million. It was quickly decided that the repairs and rebuilding would be done with traditional techniques, using original materials whenever feasible.

Dubrovnik has since regained most of its original grandeur. The town walls are once again intact, the gleaming marble streets are smoothly paved and famous monuments have been lovingly restored, with the help of an international brigade of specially trained stonemasons.

From here it's mainly downhill as you pass over Pile Gate and then narrow to single file as you climb towards **Fort Bokar** (Tvrđava Bokar) at the city's southwestern corner. The seaward stretch of the walls passes a couple of cafe-bars and souvenir stores, before terminating at Fort St John at the entrance to Dubrovnik's Old Harbour.

Fort St John

The present appearance of this massive **battlement** (Tvrđava sv Ivana) dates to the 16th century, but you may be able to spot the outline of the original square tower (built in 1346) that predated it. You can pose on cannons along the upper terrace during a city walls walk, but you'll need separate tickets to visit the attractions within.

Set in the cool stone vaults of the fort's ground floor, the **Aquarium** (Akvarij; ☎020-323 978; www.imp-du.com; Kneza Damjana Jude 12; adult/child 60/20KN; ⏰9am-7pm) makes for a pleasant escape from the scorching heat and crowds, despite being modest in content and somewhat overpriced. It's run by the University of Dubrovnik's Institute for Marine & Coastal Research, and showcases the flora and fauna of the Adriatic Sea. It also serves as a rehabilitation centre for injured sea turtles.

Up above, near the entrance to the walls, the well-presented **Maritime Museum** (Pomorski muzej; ☏020-323 904; www.dumus.hr; Tvrđava Sv Ivana; multimuseum pass adult/child 120/25KN; ⊙9am-6pm Tue-Sun Apr-Oct, to 4pm Nov-Mar) traces the history of navigation in Dubrovnik with ship models, maritime objects and paintings.

Directly next door is the **Pulitika Studio** (Atelijer Pulitika; ☏020-323 104; www.ugdubrovnik.hr; Tvrđava Sv Ivana bb; multimuseum pass adult/child 120/25KN; ⊙9am-3pm Tue-Sun), a small, cavelike space which was the workroom of painter Đuro Pulitika until his death in 2006. It looks like a moment paused in time, with his work displayed everywhere and his reading glasses casually forgotten on the side table. The larger front room often hosts exhibitions by local artists.

Fort Lawrence

St Blaise gazes down from the walls of this large, free-standing **fortress** (Tvrđava Lovrjenac; www.citywallsdubrovnik.hr; 50KN; free with city walls ticket; ⊙8am-6.30pm Apr-Oct, 9am-3pm Nov-Mar), constructed atop a 37m-high promontory adjacent to the old town. Built to

guard the city's western approach from invasion by land or sea, its walls range from 4m to 12m thick. There's not a lot inside, but the battlements offer wonderful views over the old town and its large courtyard is often used as a venue for summer theatre and concerts. Admission is included with the City Walls ticket.

Fort Revelin

The largest of the old town forts, **Revelin** (Trg Oružja) sits outside the walls, protecting the Old Harbour and the eastern approach to the city. It's part of the elaborate defensive structure of the Ploče Gate (p35). A stone bridge links it to the old town, while on the other side there's a wooden drawbridge and another stone bridge. The lower part of the fort was built in 1463, but it was enlarged considerably in 1538.

The best way to see inside is to visit the **Archaeological Museum** (Arheološki muzej; ☎020-324 041; www.dumus.hr; multimuseum pass adult/child 120/25KN; ☺10am-4pm Thu-Tue) on the ground floor. The museum presents two exhibitions, one on archaeological research pertaining to the fort and its foundry (which once produced cannons and bells), and the other on early-medieval sculpture. Among the displayed fragments of inscribed masonry, there are some good examples of medieval plait-work (*pleter*) – psychedelic

Game of Thrones

Dubrovnik's walls and forts feature prominently in the HBO series *Game of Thrones*. Fort Minčeta was used for the exterior shots of Qarth's House of the Undying, Tyrion Lannister commanded the defence of King's Landing from the seaward-facing walls during the Battle of the Blackwater and, if you can look past all of the CGI enhancements, you'll recognise Fort Lawrence as the Red Keep's core.

squiggles somewhat similar to those associated with Celtic art.

Above the museum, housed in a vast vaulted chamber, is the Revelin nightclub (p57).

Upper Corner Tower

Built in 1346, the **Upper Corner Tower** (Kula Gornji ugao; Celestina Medovića bb; 30KN; ☺8am-6.30pm Apr-Oct) is one of the 15 square towers added to the town walls in the 14th century. From the late 15th century until the devastating 1667 earthquake, the area within the walls from this tower to Fort Minčeta was the site of a foundry. After the earthquake it was filled with rubble and forgotten about, until it was uncovered during an archaeological dig in 2005. The remains of the foundry are now showcased in a snazzy museum, brought to life by multimedia displays loaded onto digital tablets.

Top Sights 📷
Srđ

From the top of this 412m-high hill, Dubrovnik's old town looks even more surreal than usual – like a scale model of itself or an illustration on a page. The views take in all of Dubrovnik and Lokrum, with the Elafiti Islands filling the horizon. It's this extraordinary vantage point that made Srđ a key battleground during the 1990s war.

Cable Car

Dubrovnik's **cable car** (Map p44, G1; Žičara; ☏ 020-414 355; www.dubrovnikcablecar.com; Petra Krešimira IV bb, Ploče; adult/child return 140/60KN, one way 85/40KN; ⏰ 9am-midnight Jun-Aug, to 10pm Sep, to 8pm Apr, May & Oct, to 4pm Nov-Mar) whisks you from just north of the city walls to the top of Srđ in under four minutes. When it was built in 1969, it was the first of its kind in the Adriatic. The large **cross** adjacent to the upper-terminus building was originally erected in 1935, sculpted from the island of Brač's famous white stone. The current cable car and cross are replacements for the originals, destroyed in 1991 during the siege of Dubrovnik. The terminus building houses a restaurant, souvenir shop, toilets and a viewing platform, with telescopes to help you pick out details far, far below.

Way of the Cross

This free alternative to the cable-car ride starts on the highway, above the old town, and terminates at Fort Imperial. The path up Srđ takes roughly an hour and is lined with highly stylised brass reliefs illustrating the 14 Stations of the Cross (a Catholic devotion depicting Jesus' journey from trial to tomb). Wear good shoes.

Dubrovnik in the Homeland War

Set inside the crumbling Napoleonic Fort Imperial (completed in 1812) near the cable-car terminus, this permanent **exhibition** (Dubrovnik u Domovinskom ratu; ☏ 020-324 856; adult/child 30/15KN; ⏰ 8am-10pm; P) is dedicated to the siege of Dubrovnik during the 'Homeland War', as the 1990s war is dubbed in Croatia. By retaining control of the fort, the local defenders ensured that the city wasn't captured. If the displays are understandably one-sided and overly wordy, they still provide in-depth coverage of the events, including video footage.

★ **Top Tips**

○ Save yourself a steep walk and 55KN by catching the cable car to the top and walking back down.

○ Try to position yourself at the city end of the cable car for the best views.

○ The cable car is closed during strong winds.

✕ **Take a Break**

You can't beat the views from **Panorama Restaurant** (www.nautikarestaurants.com; mains 88-192KN; ⏰ 9am-5pm Nov-Mar, to 9pm Apr, May, Sep & Oct, to midnight Jun-Aug; ☏), at the upper cable-car terminal, but be prepared to pay a premium.

For a traditional local grill at local prices, take a 25-minute walk down to **Konoba Dubrava** (☏ 020-416 405; www.konobadubrava.com; Bosanka bb; mains 63-159KN; ⏰ 11am-midnight; P ☏ ♿) in the neighbouring village of Bosanka.

Walking Tour 🥾

Strolling through Ploče & Viktorija

While most of suburban Dubrovnik spreads west from the walled city, its most well-heeled neighbourhoods lie immediately to the east. Grand villas and hotels sprang up here in the 1920s and '30s, taking advantage of spectacular views of the old town and some lovely beaches. A stroll along the road shadowing the coast provides a window into Dubrovnik's glitzy side.

Walk Facts

Start Pizzeria Tabasco
Finish Sveti Jakov Beach
Length 2km; one hour

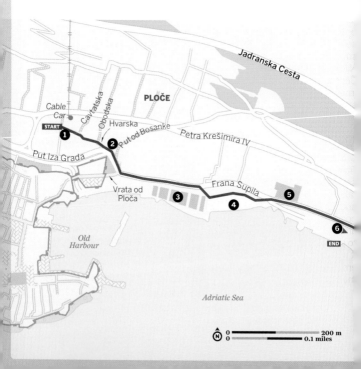

❶ Pizzeria Tabasco

Start with lunch at reasonably priced locals' hangout **Pizzeria Tabasco** (☎020-429 595; www.pizzeriatabasco.hr; Hvarska 48, Ploče; mains 40-85KN; ⏰9.30am-midnight May-Oct, to 11pm Tue-Sun Nov-Apr; ✈). Order a tasty wood-fired pizza and enjoy it sitting on one of the shady terraces hidden between the old town and the cable-car station.

❷ Kawa

Call into **Kawa** (☎091 89 67 509; www.kawa.life; Hvarska 2, Ploče; ⏰10am-8pm), a hip design store selling Croatian-designed oddities such as cushions in the shape of Nikola Tesla's head and the *Happy Ćevapi* range of T-shirts (cartoon images of gleeful-looking sausages). Stock up on domestic craft beer and wine for later.

❸ Lazareti

Drop by the **Lazareti** (www.arl.hr; Frana Supila 8, Ploče) arts centre to see what's on during your stay and take a look at its historic buildings and courtyards. This walled-in complex was built between 1590 and 1642 as a quarantine station to protect the city from the plague. It now hosts art exhibitions, cinema screenings, club nights, live music and folk dancing.

❹ Banje Beach

Take a stroll along **Banje Beach** (www.banjebeach.com; Frana Supila 10, Ploče), the busiest and most glamorous of Dubrovnik's beaches. Stop for a drink at the flash beach bar, hire a lounger or throw a towel down on the eastern end of the shingly beach for free. Late at night the bar morphs into a club.

❺ Museum of Modern Art

Visit this excellent **gallery** (Umjetnička galerija; ☎020-426 590; www.ugdubrovnik.hr; Frana Supila 23, Ploče; multimuseum pass adult/child 120/25KN; ⏰9am-8pm Tue-Sun) for its architecture and the view from the sculpture terrace, but particularly for its excellent collection of Croatian art. Built in the 1930s as a residence for a Dubrovnik shipowner, this interesting building includes elements of Modernism while tipping a hat to the Gothic and Renaissance architecture of Dubrovnik's historic core.

❻ Sveti Jakov Beach

Wander past Dubrovnik's grandest houses to the most 'local' of Dubrovnik's beaches, **Sveti Jakov Beach** (Vlaha Bukovca bb, Viktorija), positioned at the far end of the coastal strip. Take a late-afternoon swim in the deliciously clear water and stay to watch the sun set over the old town from the terrace of the beach bar.

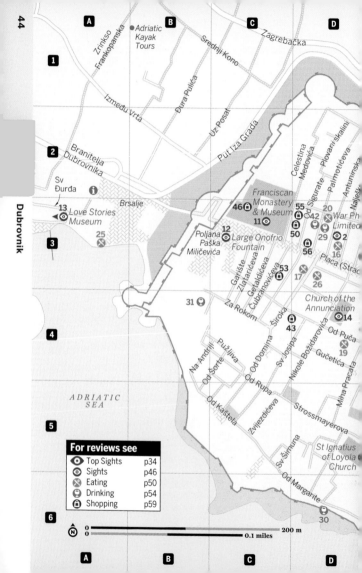

Dubrovnik

A Zrinsko Frankopanska
Adriatic Kayak Tours
B Srednji Kono
Zagrebačka
C
D

1

Izmedu Vrta
Dura Pulića
Uz Posat
Puf Iza Grada

2 Branitelja Dubrovnika
Sv Đurđa ℹ
13 Love Stories Museum
Brsalje
Celestina Medovića
Sigurate
Plovani skalini
Palmotićeva
Antuninska
Nalješk

Franciscan Monastery & Museum
46 🔒 55 🔒 20
11 👁 42 War Ph Limited
50 29 👁 2
25 ✖
12 👁 Poljana Paška Miličevića
Large Onofrio Fountain
56 16
Placa (Strac
53 ✖ 17 ✖ 26
Garište
Zlatarićeva
Getaldićeva
Čubranovićeva
Church of the Annunciation 👁 14
31 🍷 Za Rokom
Široka
43 🔒 Od Puča
19
4
Na Andriji
Pužiljiva
Od Šorte
Od Domina
Od Rupa
Sv Josipa
Nikole Božidarovića
Gučetića
Miha Pracata
Od Kaštela
Zvijezdićeva
Strossmayerova
ADRIATIC SEA
Sv Šimuna
Od Margarite
St Ignatius of Loyola Church
5
30

For reviews see
👁	Top Sights	p34
👁	Sights	p46
✖	Eating	p50
🍷	Drinking	p54
🔒	Shopping	p59

6 Ⓝ 0 _____ 200 m
0 _____ 0.1 miles

A
B
C
D

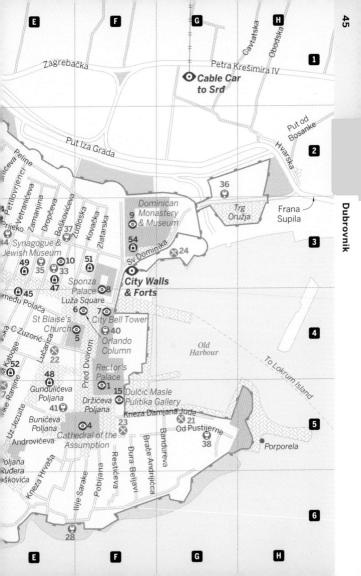

E **F** **G** **H**

1

Zagrebačka

Petra Krešimira IV

Cable Car to Srd

Put od Bosanke

2

Put Iza Grada

Hvarska

Frana Supila

3

Peline

Petilovrijenci

Vetranićeva

Zamanjina

Dropčeva

Boškovićeva

Žudioska

Kovačka

Zlatarska

36

Trg Oružja

Dominican Monastery & Museum

9

54

Sv Dominika

24

Synagogue & Jewish Museum

49 35

10

51

33

47

Sponza Palace

8

6 7

City Walls & Forts

45

medu Polača

Luža Square

St Blaise's Church

5

City Bell Tower

40

Orlando Column

Old Harbour

To Lokrum Island

4

C Zuzorić

Lučarica

52

22

Pred Dvorom

Rector's Palace

1

48

Gundulićeva Poljana

41

15

Dulčić Masle Pulitika Gallery

Držićeva Poljana

23

Kneza Damjana Jude

21

Od Pustijerne

5

Uz Jezuite

ike Ranjine

Bunićeva Poljana

4

Androvićeva

Cathedral of the Assumption

Restićeva

Pobijana

Đura Bjelavi

Bandureva

Braće Andrijića

38

Porporela

Poljana Ruđera Boškovića

Kneza Hrvaša

Ilije Sarake

28

6

E **F** **G** **H**

Museums of Dubrovnik Pass

Perhaps it's a cunning plan to get you through the doors of some of the town's more marginal museums; nine of Dubrovnik's institutions can be visited by buying a multimuseum pass (adult/child 120/25KN). The only must-see among them is the Rector's Palace, which is also the only one that can also be ticketed separately. If you're interested in visiting the excellent Museum of Modern Art (p43), then it's worth buying the pass. The other museums could easily be skipped, but if you want to get your money's worth in a limited amount of time, we suggest you prioritise the rest in the following order: Maritime Museum (p38), Archaeological Museum (p39), Dulčić Masle Pulitika Gallery (p50), Natural History Museum, Ethnographic Museum, Pulitika Studio (p38), Marin Držić House.

Sights

Rector's Palace   PALACE

1 ◉ MAP P44, F5

Built in the late 15th century for the elected rector who governed Dubrovnik, this Gothic Renaissance palace contains the rector's office and private chambers, public halls, administrative offices and a dungeon. During his one-month term the rector was unable to leave the building without the permission of the senate. Today the palace has been turned into the **Cultural History Museum**, with artfully restored rooms, portraits, coats of arms and coins, evoking the glorious history of Ragusa. (Knežev dvor; ☏020-321 497; www. dumus.hr; Pred Dvorom 3; adult/child 80/25KN, incl in multimuseum pass adult/child 120/25KN; ⏰9am-6pm Apr-Oct, to 4pm Nov-Mar)

War Photo Limited   GALLERY

2 ◉ MAP P44, D3

An immensely powerful experience, this gallery features compelling exhibitions curated by New Zealand photojournalist Wade Goddard, who worked in the Balkans in the 1990s. Its declared intention is to 'expose the myth of war...to let people see war as it is, raw, venal, frightening, by focusing on how war inflicts injustices on innocents and combatants alike'. There's a permanent exhibition on the upper floor devoted to the wars in Yugoslavia; the changing exhibitions cover a multitude of conflicts. (☏020-322 166; www. warphotoltd.com; Antuninska 6; adult/ child 50/40KN; ⏰10am-10pm May-Sep, to 4pm Wed-Mon Apr & Oct)

St Ignatius of Loyola Church   CHURCH

3 MAP P44, D5

Dramatically poised at the top of a broad flight of stairs, this Jesuit church was built in the baroque style between 1699 and 1725. Inside, magnificent frescos display scenes from the life of St Ignatius, founder of the Society of Jesus. Abutting the church is the former Jesuit college Collegium Ragusinum, today the Diocesan Classical high school. (Crkva Sv Ignacija Lojolskoga; ☏020-323 500; Poljana Ruđera Boškovića 6; ⏱7am-7pm)

Cathedral of the Assumption   CATHEDRAL

4 MAP P44, F5

Built on the site of a 7th-century basilica, Dubrovnik's original cathedral was enlarged in the 12th century, supposedly funded by a gift from England's King Richard I, the Lionheart, who was saved from a shipwreck on the nearby island of Lokrum. Soon after the first cathedral was destroyed in the 1667 earthquake, work began on this, its baroque replacement, which was finished in 1713. (Katedrala Marijina Uznesenja; Držićeva poljana; treasury 20KN; ⏱8am-5pm Mon-Sat, 11am-5pm Sun Easter-Oct, 9am-noon & 4-5pm Mon-Sat Nov-Easter)

Dubrovnik Sights

Rector's Palace

Central Swimming Spots

Dubrovnik's most glitzy beach is Banje (p43), immediately east of the old town. When locals need to cool off, they head no further than **Porporela** (Map p44, H5), the pier adjacent to Fort St John in the Old Harbour. The rocky base of Dubrovnik's formidable walls may not be the most obvious spot for a dip, but plenty of people take to the crystalline waters here. Steps lead down from both of the clifftop bars – Buža (p55) and Bard Mala Buža (p54) – and sunbathers can make use of cemented space between the rocks. In the shadow of Fort Lawrence and the surrounding cliffs, little **Šulić Bay** (Od Tabakerije 11) has showers, toilets and a cafe, and its concrete fringes are popular with sunbathers. Positioned below an old monastery at the foot of Gradac Park, 600m west of the Pile Gate, **Danče** (Don Frana Bulića bb) has turquoise waters and a series of sunbathing terraces. Further west, below the Hotel Bellevue, pebbly **Bellevue Beach** (Montovjerna) is sheltered by high cliffs.

St Blaise's Church   CHURCH

5 ◉ MAP P44, F4

Dedicated to the city's patron saint, this exceptionally beautiful church was built in 1715 in the ornate baroque style. The interior is notable for its marble altars and a 15th-century silver gilt statue of St Blaise (within the high altar) holding a scale model of pre-earthquake Dubrovnik. Note also the stained-glass windows designed by local artist Ivo Dulčić in 1971. (Crkva Sv Vlahe; Luža Sq; ⏰8am-noon & 4-5pm Mon-Sat, 7am-1pm Sun)

Orlando Column   MONUMENT

6 ◉ MAP P44, F4

Luža Sq once served as a marketplace, and this stone column – carved in 1417 and featuring the image of a medieval knight –

used to be the spot where edicts, festivities and public verdicts were announced. The knight's forearm (51.2cm) was the official linear measure of the Republic – the ell of Dubrovnik. (Orlandov stup; Luža Sq)

City Bell Tower   TOWER

7 ◉ MAP P44, F4

Marking the eastern end of the old town's main drag, this slender dome-capped tower has a large curvy clock face known as 'the octopus' and a two-tonne bell struck by two bronze jacks named Maro and Baro. (Gradski zvonik; Placa bb)

Sponza Palace   PALACE

8 ◉ MAP P44, F4

One of the few buildings in the old town to survive the 1667 earthquake, Sponza Palace was built from 1516 to 1522 as a customs house, and has subsequently been used as a mint, treasury, armoury and bank. Architecturally it's a mix of styles beginning with an exquisite Renaissance portico resting on six Corinthian columns. The 1st floor has late-Gothic windows and the 2nd-floor windows are in a Renaissance style, with an alcove containing a statue of St Blaise. (Palača Sponza; ☎020-321 031; Placa bb; May-Oct free, Nov-Apr 25KN; ⏱archives display & cloister 10am-10pm May-Oct; cloister 10am-3pm Nov-Apr)

Dominican Monastery & Museum   CHRISTIAN MONASTERY

9 ◉ MAP P44, F3

This imposing structure is an architectural highlight, built in a transitional Gothic-Renaissance style and containing an impressive art collection. Constructed around the same time as the city walls in the 14th century, the stark exterior resembles a fortress more than a religious complex. The interior contains a graceful 15th-century **cloister** constructed by local artisans after the designs of the Florentine architect Maso di Bartolomeo. (Dominikanski samostan i muzej; ☎020-321 423; www.dominicanmuseum.hr; Sv Dominika 4; adult/child 30/20KN; ⏱9am-5pm)

Synagogue & Jewish Museum   SYNAGOGUE

10 ◉ MAP P44, E3

With a religious practice that can be traced back to the 14th century, this is said to be the second-oldest still-functioning synagogue in Europe and the oldest Sephardic one. Sitting on a street that was once the Jewish ghetto, the synagogue also houses a small museum exhibiting religious relics and documentation on the local Jewish population, including records relating to their persecution during WWII. (Sinagoga i Židovski muzej; Žudioska 5; 50KN; ⏱10am-5pm)

Franciscan Monastery & Museum   CHRISTIAN MONASTERY

11 ◉ MAP P44, C3

Within this monastery's solid stone walls is a gorgeous mid-14th-century cloister, a historic pharmacy and a small museum with a collection of relics and liturgical objects, including chalices, paintings and gold jewellery, and pharmacy items such as laboratory gear and medical books. (Franjevački samostan i muzej; ☎020-321 410; Placa 2; 30KN; ⏱9am-6pm Apr-Oct, to 2pm Nov-Mar)

Large Onofrio Fountain   FOUNTAIN

12 ◉ MAP P44, C3

One of Dubrovnik's most famous landmarks, this circular fountain was built in 1438 as part of a water-supply system that involved bringing water from a spring 12km away. Originally the fountain was adorned with sculptures, but it was heavily damaged in the 1667 earthquake and only 16 carved masks remain, with their mouths dribbling drinkable water into a drainage pool. Its sibling, the ornate **Little Onofrio Fountain**, is in Luža Sq at the other end of Stradun. (Velika Onofrijeva fontana; Poljana Paska Miličevića)

Love Stories Museum MUSEUM

13 ◉ MAP P44, A3

Providing a sunny Dalmatian counterpoint to Zagreb's popular Museum of Broken Relationships, this unusual museum aims to tug at the heart strings. Exhibits focus on love songs, romantic stories from local history and legend, and smoochy scenes from films and TV series shot in Dubrovnik (*Game of Thrones* without the viscera?). However the museum's real heart is in the collection of sentimental objects donated by ordinary people and the stories behind them. (www.lovestories museum.com; Od Tabakarije 2, Pile; adult/child 50/35KN; ⏱9am-10pm May-Sep, 10am-6pm Oct-Apr)

Church of the Annunciation CHURCH

14 ◉ MAP P44, D4

The old town's sole Serbian Orthodox church provides an interesting contrast to the numerous Catholic churches scattered about. Dating from 1877, it suffered substantial damage during the most recent war and was only fully restored in 2009. (Crkva sv Blagovještenja; ☏020-323 283; Od Puča 8; ⏱8am-7.30pm Apr-Jun, Sep & Oct, to 10pm Jul & Aug, to 6pm Nov-Mar)

Dulčić Masle Pulitika Gallery GALLERY

15 ◉ MAP P44, F5

This small offshoot of the city's main gallery unites three friends beyond the grave: local artists Ivo Dulčić, Antun Masle and Đuro Pulitika, who all came to the fore in the 1950s and 1960s. There's a permanent collection featuring the trio's work on the lower floor, while the upper gallery is given over to temporary exhibitions by current artists. (☏020-612 645; www.ugdu brovnik.hr; Držićeva poljana 1; multi-museum pass adult/child 120/25KN; ⏱9am-8pm Tue-Sun)

Eating

Dolce Vita SWEETS $

16 ✖ MAP P44, D3

Over a dozen different kinds of sumptuous, creamy gelato are on offer at this sweet spot. Alternatively, choose from a substantial menu of cakes and pancakes. You'll have no trouble finding it, as its bright orange chairs and lanterns picturing an ice-cream cone pop out from a narrow side street just off Stradun. (Nalješkovićeva 1a; ice cream/pancakes from 11/22KN; ⏱11am-midnight)

Fast Food Republic FAST FOOD $

17 ✖ MAP P44, D3

Owned and operated by a friendly young crew, this little burger bar serves a tasty selection of burgers, sandwiches, pizza slices and hot dogs. For a local twist, try an octopus burger. (www.facebook.com/RepublicDubrovnik; Široka 4; mains 39-100KN; ⏲10am-midnight; 🛜)

Pink Shrimp
SEAFOOD $

18 ✂ MAP P44, D3

This petite streetside eatery highlights its namesake, one of the key Dalmatian ingredients, preparing it in a dozen different ways, including tartare, tempura, fried, in salad and on bruschetta. Coupled with a simple yet striking wine list, the menu at Pink Shrimp makes for a tasty light lunch or evening snack option. Leave room for the chocolate mousse. (www.facebook.com/PinkShrimpStreetFood; Kunićeva 2; dishes 44-86KN; ⏲10am-midnight)

Peppino's
ICE CREAM $

19 ✂ MAP P44, D4

With over 20 tempting varieties of thick, delicious gelato on offer, this artisanal ice-cream shop serves everything from your standard chocolate to funky remakes based on popular candy or cakes. The premium ice cream has an even richer flavour, and gluten-free scoops are also available. (www.peppinos.premis.hr; Od Puča 9; scoops from 14KN; ⏲11am-midnight)

Nishta
VEGAN $$

20 ✂ MAP P44, D3

The popularity of this tiny old-town restaurant is testament not just to the paucity of options for vegetarians and vegans in Croatia, but also to the imaginative and

Republic of Ragusa

The story of Dubrovnik begins with the 7th-century onslaught of the Slavs, which had wiped out the Roman city of Epidaurum (present-day Cavtat). Residents fled to the safest place they could find, which was the rocky islet of Ragusa, separated from the mainland by a narrow channel. Building walls was a matter of pressing urgency due to the threat of invasion; the city was well fortified by the 9th century when it resisted a Saracen siege for 15 months.

Meanwhile, another settlement emerged on the mainland, which became known as Dubrovnik, named after the *dubrava* (holm oak) that carpeted the region. The two settlements merged in the 12th century, and the channel that separated them was filled in.

By the end of the 12th century Dubrovnik had become a significant trading centre on the coast, providing an important link between the Mediterranean and Balkan states. Dubrovnik came under Venetian authority in 1205, finally breaking away from its control in 1358.

By the 15th century the Respublica Ragusina (Republic of Ragusa) had extended its borders to include the entire coastal belt from Ston to Cavtat, having previously acquired Lastovo Island, the Pelješac Peninsula and Mljet Island. It was now a force to be reckoned with. The city turned towards sea trade and established a fleet of its own ships, which were dispatched to Egypt, the Levant, Sicily, Spain, France and Istanbul. Through canny diplomacy the city maintained good relations with everyone – even the Ottoman Empire, to which Dubrovnik began paying tribute in the 16th century.

Centuries of peace and prosperity allowed art, science and literature to flourish, but most of the Renaissance art and architecture in Dubrovnik was destroyed in the earthquake of 1667, which killed 5000 people and left the city in ruins. Holy Saviour Church, the Sponza Palace and the Rector's Palace are the only significant buildings remaining from before this time. The earthquake also marked the beginning of the economic decline of the town.

The final coup de grâce was dealt by Napoleon, whose troops entered Dubrovnik in 1808 and announced the end of the republic. The Vienna Congress of 1815 ceded Dubrovnik to Austria; though the city maintained its shipping, it succumbed to social disintegration. Following WWI the city started to develop its tourist industry, swiftly becoming Yugoslavia's leading attraction.

beautifully presented food produced within. Each day of the week has its own menu with a separate set of cooked and raw options. (📞020-322 088; www.nishtarestaurant.com; Prijeko bb; mains 98-108KN; 🕙11.30am-11.30pm Mon-Sat; 🍴)

Konoba Ribar DALMATIAN $$

21 MAP P44, G5

A rarity for the old town, this little family-run spot serves local food the way locals like it, at more-or-less local prices. It doesn't attempt anything fancy or clever, just big serves of traditional favourites such as risotto and stuffed squid drenched in olive oil and garlic. It's set in a little lane pressed hard up against the city walls. (📞020-323 194; Kneza Damjana Jude bb; mains 85-130KN; 🕙10am-11pm; 📶)

Oliva Pizzeria PIZZA $$

22 MAP P44, E4

There are a few token pasta dishes on the menu, but this attractive little restaurant is really all about pizza. And the pizza is worthy of the attention. Grab a seat on the street and tuck in. (📞020-324 594; www.pizza-oliva.com; Lučarica 5; mains 74-105KN; 🕙10am-11pm; 📶🍴)

Bota Šare Oyster & Sushi Bar SUSHI $$

23 MAP P44, F5

It's fair to say that most Croatians don't have much of an interest in or aptitude for Asian cooking, yet fresh seafood is something

that they understand very well, as this little place demonstrates. Grab a terrace table with a view of the cathedral and tuck into Ston oysters (fresh or tempura style) and surprisingly good sushi and sashimi. (📞020-324 034; www.bota-sare.hr; Od Pustijerne bb; mains 62-120KN; 🕙noon-midnight)

Restaurant 360° INTERNATIONAL $$$

24 MAP P44, G3

Dubrovnik's glitziest restaurant offers fine dining at its best, with flavoursome, beautifully presented, creative cuisine, an impressive wine list and slick, professional service. The setting is unrivalled – on top of the city walls with tables positioned so you can peer through the battlements over the harbour. (📞020-322 222; www.360dubrovnik.com; Sv Dominika bb; 2/3/5 courses 520/620/860KN; 🕙6.30-10.30pm Tue-Sun Apr-Sep; 📶)

Nautika EUROPEAN $$$

25 MAP P44, A3

Nautika bills itself as 'Dubrovnik's finest restaurant' and it comes pretty close. The setting is sublime, overlooking the sea and the city walls, and the service is faultless: black bow-tie formal but friendly. As for the food, it's sophisticated if not particularly adventurous, with classic techniques applied to the finest local produce. For maximum silver-service drama, order the salt-crusted fish. (📞020-442 526; www.nautikarestaurants.com; Brsalje 3,

Kayak Tours

You can't beat a kayak trip for confronting the daunting scale of Dubrovnik's sea walls. Sunset tours are particularly popular. **Adriatic Kayak Tours** (Map p44, B1; 020-312 770; www.adriatickayaktours.com; Zrinsko Frankopanska 6, Pile; half-day from 280KN; Apr-Oct) and **Outdoor Croatia** (020-418 282; www.outdoorcroatia.com; day trip 440KN) both offer paddle-powered expeditions.

Pile; mains 290-360KN; 6pm-midnight Apr-Oct)

Proto   SEAFOOD $$$

26 MAP P44, D3

This elegant place is known for its fresh fish and bags of old-town atmosphere. To say it's 'long-standing' is an understatement – it opened its doors in 1886 and has served the likes of Edward VIII and Wallis Simpson. The menu show-cases Dalmatian and Istrian cuisine, including fresh pasta, grilled fish and a few token meat dishes. (020-323 234; www.esculaprestaurants.com; Široka 1; mains 225-356KN; 10.30am-11pm)

Restaurant Dubrovnik   EUROPEAN $$$

27 MAP P44, E5

One of Dubrovnik's most upmarket restaurants has a wonderfully unstuffy setting, occupying a covered rooftop terrace hidden among the venerable stone buildings of the old town. A strong French influence pervades a menu full of decadent and rich dishes, such as confit duck and perfectly cooked steak. (020-324 810; www.restorandubrovnik.com; Marojice Kaboge 5; mains 110-230KN; noon-midnight;)

Drinking

Bard Mala Buža   BAR

28 P44, E6

The more upmarket and slick of two cliff bars pressed up against the seaward side of the city walls. This one is lower on the rocks and has a shaded terrace where you can lose a day quite happily, mesmerised by the Adriatic vistas. (Iza Mira 14; 9am-3am May-Oct)

D'vino   WINE BAR

29 MAP P44, D3

If you're interested in sampling top-notch Croatian wine, this convivial bar is the place to go. As well as a large and varied wine list, it offers tasting flights presented by cool and knowledge-able staff (three wines from 55KN) plus savoury breakfasts, snacks and platters. Sit outside for the authentic old-town-alley ambience, but check out the whimsical wall inscriptions inside. (020-321 130; www.dvino.net; Palmotićeva 4a; 9am-midnight Mar-Nov;)

Buža

BAR

30  MAP P44, D6

Finding this ramshackle bar-on-a-cliff feels like a real discovery as you duck and dive around the city walls and finally see the entrance tunnel. However, Buža's no secret – it gets insanely busy, especially around sunset. Wait for a space on one of the concrete platforms, grab a cool drink in a plastic cup and enjoy the vibe and views. (off Od Margarite; ⏱8am-2am Jun-Aug, to midnight Sep-May)

Tavulin

WINE BAR

31  MAP P44, B4

Claiming a relatively quiet corner of the old town, this cute little 'wine and art bar' pours a plethora of wine by the glass, sourced from all over the country. (📞099 88 54 197; www.facebook.com/Tavulin ArtWine; Za Rokom 11; ⏱10.30am-10pm; 📶)

Dubrovnik Beer Factory

CRAFT BEER

32  MAP P44, D4

The name might mislead you: this isn't, in fact, a brewery, but the selection of Croatian craft beer is good enough to justify the tag. Still, with huge murals, vaulted ceilings, historic stone details and a large beer garden tucked away in the back, the setting remains the true drawcard. It also serves food and hosts live music. (www.facebook.com/dubrovnikbeerfactory; Miha Pracata 6; ⏱9am-1am; 📶)

Bard Mala Buža

SANDRA MORI/SHUTTERSTOCK ©

Cavtat

Set on a petite peninsula embraced by two harbours, the ancient town of Cavtat (pronounced *tsav*-tat) has a pretty waterfront promenade peppered with restaurants, pebbly beaches and an interesting assortment of artsy attractions.

Founded in the 6th century BC as a Greek settlement called Epidaurus, Cavtat became a Roman colony in 228 BC and was subsequently destroyed by invading Avars and Slavs in the 7th century. Re-established in the Middle Ages under the Republic of Ragusa (Dubrovnik), it shared in the cultural and economic life of the nearby capital. The walls of its famous offshoot are visible in the distance and the two are well connected by both boat and bus, making Cavtat an easy day-trip destination.

Bukovac House (Kuća Bukovac; 020-478 646; www.kuca-bukovac. hr; Bukovčeva 5; 30KN; 9am-6pm Mon-Sat, to 2pm Sun Apr-Oct, 10am-6pm Tue-Sat, 9am-1pm Sun Nov-Mar) is where Cavtat's most famous son, the painter Vlaho Bukovac (1855–1922), was born and raised. It has been converted into an interesting little museum devoted to his work. The early-19th-century architecture provides a fitting backdrop to his mementoes, drawings and paintings. You'll see more of his works in **St Nicholas' Church** (Crkva svetog Nikole; Obala Ante Starčevića bb; hours vary) and the **Our-Lady-of-the-Snow Monastery** (Samostan Gospe od snijega; 020-678 064; www.franjevacki-sam ostan-cavtat.com; Šetalište Rat 2; 7am-9pm).

Completed in 1921, the octagonal white-stone **Račić Family Mausoleum** (Mauzolej obitelji Račić; www.migk.hr; Groblje sv Roka, Kvaternikova bb; 20KN; 10am-5pm Mon-Sat Apr-Oct) is the handiwork of pre-eminent Croatian sculptor Ivan Meštrović. Inside a heavenly host of angelic faces gaze down on stylised saints. You'll find it in the town cemetery, in the wooded area near the end of the peninsula.

Not just the best place to eat on Cavtat's seafront strip, **Bugenvila** (020-479 949; www.bugenvila.eu; Obala Ante Starčevića 9; mains 90-275KN; noon-4pm & 6.30-10pm;) is one of the culinary trendsetters of the Dalmatian coast. Local ingredients are showcased in adventurous dishes served with artistic flourishes.

During the tourist season at least three different operators offer boats to Cavtat from Dubrovnik's Old Harbour (one way/return 100/60KN, 45 minutes), with departures at least every half hour (reduced in winter). Bus 10 runs roughly half-hourly to Cavtat (25KN, 30 minutes) from Dubrovnik.

Rock Caffe Exit   BAR

33 🚇 MAP P44, E3

Favoured by local rockers and metalheads, this little wood-lined upstairs bar hosts regular live acts. At other times, it's a surprisingly pleasant place for a quiet drink, away from the main tourist scrum. (Boškovićeva 3; ⏰6pm-2am)

Buzz Bar   BAR

34 🚇 MAP P44, E3

Appropriately named, this buzzy little bar is rocky and relaxed, with craft beer and cocktails being the main poisons – aside from those being exhaled by the recalcitrant smokers in the corner. (📞020-321 025; www.thebuzzbar.wixsite.com/buzz; Prijeko 21; ⏰8am-2am; 📶)

Malvasija   WINE BAR

35 🚇 MAP P44, E3

Named after the white wine produced in the neighbouring Konavle region, this tiny bar is a good spot to sample the local drop. The delicious cheese and charcuterie platters (from 80KN) are a great option for a light, affordable meal in the often-pricey old town. The service is as charming as it is knowledgeable. (Dropčeva 4; ⏰5pm-1am; 📶)

Revelin   CLUB

36 🚇 MAP P44, G2

Housed within the vast vaulted chambers of Fort Revelin, this is Dubrovnik's most impressive club space, with famous international

Cavtat harbour

Art Cafe

Dubrovnik's most bohemian cafe-bar has seats constructed from bathtubs, tables made from washing-machine agitators, brightly coloured walls, funky music and terraces front and rear. A popular daytime coffee and smoothie spot, the **Art Cafe** (☎020-311 097; www.facebook.com/ArtCafeDubrovnik; Branitelja Dubrovnika 25, Pile; ⊙9am-2am May-Sep, to midnight Mon-Thu, to 2am Fri & Sat Oct-Apr; ☎) fires up on weekend nights and delivers club-like parties. You'll find it on the main road, 400m west of the Pile Gate.

DJs dropping in during summer. (www.clubrevelin.com; Sv Dominika 3; ⊙11pm-6am daily Jun-Sep, Sat Oct-May)

Matuško   WINE BAR

37 🚇 MAP P44, E3

An outpost of the largest winery (p76) on the Pelješac Peninsula, this swanky little wine bar offers an opportunity to sample some of Croatia's acclaimed Dingač and Postup reds in an atmospheric, almost cave-like setting. (☎099 80 70 802; www.facebook.com/WineBarMatusko; Prijeko 6; ⊙10am-1am Jul-Sep, to 10pm Apr-Jun & Oct-Dec; ☎)

Cogito   CAFE

38 🚇 MAP P44, G5

Serious coffee devotees should seek out this diminutive branch of Zagreb's premier roasters, hidden under an arch on the way to the Maritime Museum. The lightly roasted blend is fruity and robust but at 35KN for a flat white, you won't be ordering a second cup. Cold brew and fresh juices are also available. (www.cogitocoffee.com; Od Pustijerne 1; ⊙9am-7pm; ☎)

Gaffe   IRISH PUB

39 🚇 MAP P44, D4

With an authentically pub-like interior and a covered side terrace, plus Guinness, O'Hara stout and Westons cider on tap, this is always the busiest place in town when there's rugby on. At other times, call in for happy hour, the easygoing menu of bar foods and grilled meats, and live music performances happening every night in summer. (☎020-332 970; www.facebook.com/irishpubthegaffe; Miha Pracata 4; ⊙9am-2am Jun-Oct, to midnight Nov-May; ☎)

Gradska kavana Arsenal   CAFE

40 🚇 MAP P44, F4

Locals come here to gossip about the news of the day or for business meetings, while travellers come for the location and the views. Chandeliers illuminate the Viennese-style interior, while the front terrace overlooks lively Luža Sq, making it ideal for people-watching. Despite the steep prices, this place is always busy. Food is served throughout the day. (☑020-321 202; www.nautikarestaurants.com; Pred Dvorom 1; ⏱8am-11pm; 📶)

Troubadour

BAR

41 🔵 MAP P44, E5

Tucked into a corner behind the cathedral, Troubadour looks pretty nondescript during the day. That all changes on summer nights, when jazz musicians set up outside and quickly draw the crowds. (☑020-323 796; www.troubadourjazzcafe.placeweb.site; Bunićeva poljana 2; ⏱7.30am-2am May-Sep, 9am-midnight Oct-Apr; 📶)

Glam Beer Therapy

CRAFT BEER

42 🔵 MAP P44, D3

This little cafe-bar is the best place in Dubrovnik to sample a selection of Croatian craft beer. (☑091 15 18 257; www.facebook.com/glamdu; Palmotićeva 5; ⏱9am-midnight Nov-May, to 2am Jun-Oct; 📶)

Shopping

Terra Croatica Dubrovnik

GIFTS & SOUVENIRS

43 🔒 MAP P44, D4

A welcome interlude in a streak of shops with cheesy souvenirs and *Game of Thrones* paraphernalia, Terra Croatica wears its Authentically Croatian Souvenir certification proudly. Pop in for gift-sized foodie treats like olive oils, wines,

Placa and the Franciscan Monastery & Museum (p49)

Konavle

After the dry and rugged coast around Dubrovnik, the lush fields and orderly vineyards of Konavle are quite a surprise. Here, in this hidden nook between the Bosnian and Montenegrin borders, east of Cavtat, the mountains have taken half a step back, providing an imposing backdrop to the fertile agricultural region. It's best known for *malvasija*, an endemic grape producing a very pleasant white wine.

There's no better place to soak up the scenery than the terrace of the exceptional family-run **Konoba Koraćeva Kuća** (020-791 557; www.koracevakuca.com; Gruda 155; mains 75-165KN; 4-10pm Mon-Fri, noon-10pm Sat & Sun mid-Apr–May, 4-10pm Jun–mid-Oct;), specialising in modern takes on Dalmatian traditions. Call ahead for lamb or veal slow-roasted under a *peka* (coal-covered metal dome), or just call in to see what's on the menu.

Perched atop a 25m-high crag, the fairy-tale castle **Sokol Grad** (020-638 800; www.citywallsdubrovnik.hr; Dunave; adult/child 70/30KN; 10am-6pm Apr-Oct, 10am-4pm Nov, noon-3pm Dec-Mar) has a name which literally means 'Falcon Town', and it certainly provides a bird's-eye view of Konavle. Built to guard one of the historic routes leading through the mountains to Hercegovina, the site has been occupied from prehistoric times, with the Romans, Byzantines and various medieval states taking turns to hold it before Dubrovnik wrested control. Restored and partly reconstructed, it now houses interesting displays on medieval weaponry and the castle's history.

Hidden below high cliffs, **Pasjača** is one of Dalmatia's most beautiful beaches, with intensely blue and green water lapping at a pebbly shore. It's a little hard to find; head to Popovići and then follow your nose along the narrow village road, keeping an eye out for the few signs pointing the way. From the parking area, a path heads along sheer cliffs and partially through tunnels carved through the rock.

Konavle is best explored by car or bike as public transport is limited. City buses 11 and 38 head from Dubrovnik to Gruda (three or four daily), or there's bus 31 from Cavtat (three to five daily). For Sokol Grad, catch bus 25 from Dubrovnik (three daily).

truffles and gourmet chocolates, but also for handmade ceramics, stone mortars, cosmetics and Dalmatian cookbooks. (020-323 209; www.facebook.com/terracroatica. dubrovnik; Od Puča 17; 9am-9pm)

Medusa

GIFTS & SOUVENIRS

44 🔒 MAP P44, E3

This self-described 'charming shop for charming people' sells locally produced soaps, flavoured salt, *rakija* (grappa), neckties, objects made from Brač stone, art prints, chocolate and toiletries. (📞020-322 004; www.medusa. hr; Prijeko 18; ⏰9am-10pm Apr-Oct, 10am-5pm Nov-Mar)

Uje

FOOD & DRINKS

45 🔒 MAP P44, E4

Uje specialises in olive oils, along with a wide range of other locally produced epicurean delights, including some excellent jams, pickled capers, local herbs and spices, honey, figs in honey, chocolate, wine and *rakija* (grappa). There's another **branch** (📞020-324 865; Od Puča 2; ⏰9am-9pm Sep-Jun, to midnight Jul & Aug) around the corner. (📞020-321 532; www.uje.hr; Placa 5; ⏰11am-6pm Jan-Mar, 9am-9pm Apr, May & Oct-Dec, 9am-11pm Jun-Sep)

Little Brothers Pharmacy

COSMETICS

46 🔒 MAP P44, C3

Call into the Franciscan monastery for the novelty of shopping at the third-oldest still-functioning pharmacy in Europe. It's been in business since 1317 and as well as all the usual stuff, it sells a range of moisturisers made from local herbs. (Ljekarna kod Mala Braća; 📞020-321 411; www.ljekarna-dubrovnik.hr; Placa 2; ⏰7am-7pm Mon-Fri, 7.30am-3pm Sat)

Dubrovnik Shopping

Large Onofrio Fountain (p49)

Elafiti Islands

A day trip to the islands in this archipelago, northwest of Dubrovnik, makes a perfect escape from the summer crowds. Out of 14 islands only the three largest are permanently inhabited. You can see all three in one day on a 'Three Islands & Picnic' tour, which is offered by various operators that have desks at Dubrovnik's Old Harbour (expect to pay between 250KN and 300KN, including drinks and lunch). Alternatively, there are regular ferries to the Elafitis from Dubrovnik's Gruž Harbour.

The nearest to Dubrovnik, sweet little **Koločep** is inhabited by a mere 163 people and is covered in centuries-old pine forests, olive groves, and orchards filled with orange and lemon trees. A sandy beach stretches out from the main village past a large resort-style hotel. Continue around the corner and you'll reach a pretty but rocky nudist area.

Car-free **Lopud** has an attractive town composed of stone houses surrounded by exotic gardens and overlooked by ruined fortresses. The first sight while sailing into the harbour is the immense seawall and 30m-high bell tower of its 15th-century **Franciscan Monastery** (Franjevački samostan; Lopud; ⊙hours vary). The only part of the complex which is regularly open to the people is St Mary-of-the-Cave Church, built in 1483 and worth a visit for its 16th-century altar piece and intricately carved choir chairs. Further along the seaside promenade is shady **Đorđić-Mayneri Park** (Obala Iva Kuljevana 31, Lopud), laid out in the late 19th century by the great-granddaughter of Dubrovnik's last rector. Botanical specimens from around the world include North African date palms, North American magnolias and Tasmanian eucalyptus trees. There's a little beach in the town, but you're better off walking across the spine of the island to sandy **Šunj**. The walk takes about 25 minutes, or you can grab a ride in a golf cart for around 20KN.

At 16 sq km, **Šipan** is the largest of the Elafiti Islands and was a favourite with the Dubrovnik aristocracy who built houses here. Most ferries dock in **Suđurađ**, a little harbour lined with stone houses and the large fortified Skočibuha villa and tower, built in the 16th century (not open to the public). On the other side of the island, the village of **Šipanska Luka** has the remains of a Roman villa and a 15th-century Gothic duke's palace. Buses, mainly timed around the ferries, connect the two settlements.

Algebra   BOOKS

47 🔒 MAP P44, E3

Among Croatian literature stacked floor-to-ceiling, this bookworm's treasure trove stocks guides, regional history books and international best-sellers in foreign languages. Plus there's an eclectic range of souvenirs, from cool postcards to decorative handmade carnival masks. Ask the wonderful staff to help you navigate, as they seem to know most of the books inside out. (📞020-323 217; www.knjizara-algebra.hr; Placa 9; ⏰8.30am-8pm)

Grad Market   MARKET

48 🔒 MAP P44, E5

Stallholders sell mainly produce, local artisanal products and crafts at this open-air market. In summer traditional craft sellers stick around until late afternoon. (www.sanitat.hr; Gundulićeva poljana; ⏰6am-2pm May-Oct, to noon Nov-Apr)

Bonbonnière Kraš   FOOD & DRINKS

49 🔒 MAP P44, E3

Prominently positioned on Dubrovnik's main street, Bonbonnière Kraš is a delight for anyone with a sweet tooth. Walls are lined with pralines, candy, chocolate, cookies and liquors, and mainly feature products by Kraš, the iconic Croatian chocolate factory established in 1911. If you're looking for an authentically Croatian sweet to take home, look no further than Bajadera nougats. (📞020-321 049; www.kras.hr; Zamanjina 2; ⏰8am-9pm)

Lopud, Elafiti Islands

Game of Thrones Locations

Dubrovnik is like a fantasy world for most people, but fans of *Game of Thrones* have more reason to indulge in flights of fancy than most, as a large chunk of the immensely popular TV series was filmed here. While Split and Šibenik were also used as locations, Dubrovnik has featured the most prominently, standing in for the cities of King's Landing and Qarth. If you fancy taking your own Walk of Shame through the streets of Westeros, here are some key spots (see also p39).

Fort Lawrence King's Landing's famous Red Keep. Cersei farewelled her daughter Myrcella from the little harbour beneath it.

Rector's Palace The atrium featured as the palace of the Spice King of Qarth – they didn't even bother moving the statue!

Sv Dominika street The street and staircase outside the Dominican Monastery were used for various King's Landing market scenes.

Uz Jezuite The stairs connecting the St Ignatius of Loyola Church to Gundulićeva poljana were the starting point for Cersei Lannister's memorable naked penitential walk. The walk continued down Stradun.

Dubrovnik Treasures JEWELLERY

50 🔒 MAP P44, D3

An Aussie-born, Croatian-bred, locally based brother-and-sister team is behind this treasure trove of very cool, well-crafted, handmade, contemporary jewellery. (📞020-321 098; www.dubrovnik treasures.com; Celestina Medovića 2; ⏰9am-8pm Mar-Nov)

Croatian Fashion Design FASHION & ACCESSORIES

51 🔒 MAP P44, F3

Tightly packed with women's clothing, accessories and jewellery, this is your window to the world of established and upcoming Croatian fashion designers. Look for designs by Igor Dobranić, whose casual and stylish items made of natural materials have already conquered the international fashion scene. (Modni Kantun; 📞098 500 377; Zlatarska 3; ⏰9am-9pm)

Romana Atelier ART

52 🔒 MAP P44, E4

A showcase for the colourful Dubrovnik-themed canvases (and painting-inspired souvenirs) of local artist Romana Milutin. (📞091 50 13 318; www.romana-milutin.com; Marojice Kaboge bb; ⏰10am-1pm & 5-9pm Mon-Sat Apr-Oct)

Talir ART

53 🔒 MAP P44, C3

Original artworks by established local artists are presented in two spaces sitting across the street from one another. (📞020-323 293; Čubranovićeva 7; 🕐9am-10pm May-Oct, 10am-7pm Nov-Apr)

Sebastian Art ART

54 🔒 MAP P44, F3

The interior of the 15th-century St Sebastian Church is the backdrop for displays of Croatian art in various forms, from sculpture to paintings and prints. Original works by both established and up-and-coming Croatian artists, replicas of national heritage, plus occasional exhibitions all adorn these ancient walls. International shipping can be arranged. (Sv Dominika 5; 🕐9am-9pm)

Stjepko Art ART

55 🔒 MAP P44, D3

Colourful canvases featuring fish and Dubrovnik scenes are the hallmarks of local artist Stjepko Mamić, as featured in this little commercial gallery and atelier. He is around more often than not, but call ahead to be sure. (📞095 90 61 703; www.raguza.net; Celestina Medovića 2; 🕐hours vary)

Vina Miličić WINE

56 🔒 MAP P44, D3

A good representation of local varieties produced by the Miličić winery sits bottle-to-bottle with champagne, sparkling wines and top-shelf liquor. (📞020-321 777; www.vinamilicic.com; Od Sigurate 2; 🕐9am-10pm May-Sep, 9am-7pm Mon-Sat, 10am-4pm Sun Apr & Oct, 9am-3pm Mon-Sat Nov-Mar)

Worth a Trip 🔭
Lokrum Island

Leave the crush of Dubrovnik's old town a world away with a 10-minute ferry ride to this lush, forested island populated by preening peacocks and over 150 other bird species. The entire island is a protected nature reserve, full of holm oaks, black ash, pines and olive trees. It's a popular swimming destination, although the beaches are rocky.

📞 020-311 738

www.lokrum.hr

adult/child incl boat
150/25KN

🕐 Apr-Nov

Benedictine Monastery & Gardens

The island's main hub is its large medieval Benedictine monastery, located a short stroll from the ferry wharf. It's thought that monks first settled on the island in the early 10th century. The last monks were eventually turfed out in 1799, when the cash-strapped republic decided to sell the island to raise funds.

Lokrum eventually fell into the hands of ill-fated Austrian Archduke Maximilian Ferdinand, the future Emperor of Mexico, who had a summer villa built within the monastery complex in the early 1860s. Maximilian was responsible for reviving the gorgeous cloister garden and planting a significant botanical garden, featuring giant agaves and exotic palms.

One of the monastery buildings now contains a display on the island's history and the TV show *Game of Thrones*. This is your chance to pose imperiously on a reproduction of the Iron Throne. Fans of the show may recognise the cloister garden as the location used for filming the reception for Daenerys in Qarth.

Fort Royal

Near the centre of the island, at its highest point (97m), is circular Fort Royal. Napoleon's troops started construction of the fort shortly after taking control of Dubrovnik in 1806. Head up to the roof for views over the old town.

Swimming Spots

The island is mainly surrounded by flat rocky ledges rather than beaches, and most visitors are content to seek a quiet shelf on which to spread out. Another popular place for a swim is the small saltwater lake known as the **Dead Sea**, south of the monastery. There's a nudist area near the southeastern tip of the island; head left from the ferry. The rocky area at its far end is Dubrovnik's de facto gay beach.

★ Top Tips

o Make sure you check what time the last boat to the mainland departs.

o The last few boats for the day can get very crowded; to guarantee a place, make sure you get to the wharf early.

o No one is allowed to stay on the island overnight.

o Smoking is not permitted anywhere on the island.

✗ Take a Break

The best place to eat on Lokrum is upmarket **Lacroma Restaurant** (www.lacroma.restaurant), situated near the Benedictine monastery. Lacroma also operates a snack bar close to the ferry wharf.

★ Getting There

Boats leave from Dubrovnik's Old Harbour roughly hourly in summer (half-hourly in July and August).

Walking Tour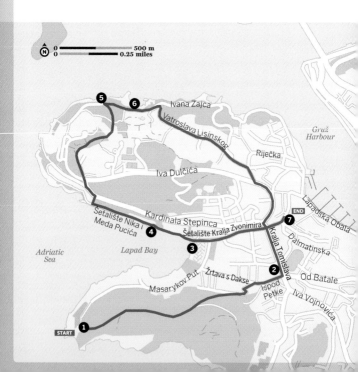

Beach-Hopping in Lapad

Despite the presence of various large resort complexes hugging the coast, the hilly Lapad Peninsula retains a much more lived-in feeling than the rest of Dubrovnik. Local families flock to the casual cafe-bars and pizzerias lining Šetalište Kralja Zvonimira, the buzzy pine-shaded pedestrian promenade leading to pretty Lapad Bay, all year round.

Walk Facts

Start Velika & Mala Petka Forest Park

Finish Shizuku

Length 5.5km, two hours

1 Velika & Mala Petka Forest Park

Start with a morning stroll through this shady 43-hectare **park** (Park-Šuma Velika i Mala Petka; off Ivanska bb) encompassing the big and little Petka hills. Few tourists make their way up here; you're unlikely to encounter more than a handful of local joggers and people walking their dogs.

2 Pantarul

Stop for lunch at this bright and breezy neighbourhood **bistro** (020-333 486; www.pantarul.com; Kralja Tomislava 1; mains 108-180KN; 5-course tasting menus 390-410KN; noon-4pm & 6pm-midnight Tue-Sun; P) but don't be fooled by the casual vibe: this is one of Dubrovnik's very best restaurants. The homemade bread and pasta are superb.

3 Lapad Bay

Follow the buzzy cafe-lined pedestrian strip down to the clear waters of **Lapad Bay** (Uvala Lapad;) and one of Dubrovnik's most family-friendly beaches. Local kids race around the park and splash about on the inflatable floating playground. Facing due west, it's a popular spot to watch the sun set over the water and Koločep Island.

4 Cave Bar More

Situated on the walkway that traces the northern edge of the bay, this **beach bar** (www.hotel -more.hr; Šetalište Nika i Meda Pucića bb, Babin Kuk; 10am-midnight Jun-Aug, to 10pm Sep-May) has a sunny terrace by the water but make sure you head into the natural cave itself, where drinks are served in the cool depths of a stalactite-filled cavern.

5 Coral Beach Club

Across the other side of the Babin Kuk hill, **Coral** (www.coral-beach -club.com; Ivana Zajca 30, Babin Kuk; 9am-9pm May–mid-Sep;) is the peninsula's ritziest locale for lazing on loungers, drinking cocktails and cooling off in the crystalline sea.

6 Copacabana Beach

Less upmarket than its neighbour, **Copacabana** (www.thebeach dubrovnik.com; Ivana Zajca bb, Babin Kuk) also has loungers, bars, a restaurant and masseurs at hand, but there's more room to spread out your towel on the pebbles and splash about in the water with the kids.

7 Shizuku

Finish your beach day with a delectable sashimi platter at Dalmatia's best Japanese **restaurant** (020-311 493; www.facebook.com/ ShizukuDubrovnik; Kneza Domagoja 1f, Batala; mains 70-85KN; 5pm-midnight Tue-Sun;), tucked away in an unassuming set of neighbourhood shops at the centre of the peninsula. Wash it down with local wine, Japanese beer or sake.

Explore ⊛

Dalmatian Coast

The coast of mainland Dalmatia is a stretch to be savoured by beach seekers, wine lovers and history buffs alike. All along its length, rugged mountains form a dramatic backdrop to a string of historic towns and beautiful pebbly beaches. Although tourism is in full swing here, there's still plenty of lush Mediterranean greenery to enjoy, including pine forests, olive groves, vineyards and orchards.

Ideally you would throw in some beach time and stretch out your stay over a few days, but you can still see a lot on a single day's drive up the coast. Start at Trsteno Arboretum (p75) then continue up the highway as far as the Pelješac Peninsula, turning off towards Ston. After exploring the walls (p72), stop for an oyster-filled lunch at Kapetanova Kuća (p73). Continue along the peninsula, pausing for a wine tasting (p76) on your way to the car ferry at Trpanj. Try to squeeze in a quick swim and look around Makarska before hitting Omiš in time for dinner.

Getting There & Around

🚌 Coaches traverse the coast between Dubrovnik and Split regularly. Some turn inland and travel down the Pelješac Peninsula.

⛴ Car ferries head between Orebić and Korčula, Makarska and Brač, and Drvenik and Hvar. From June to September, catamarans also stop in Makarska en route between Split, Bol, Korčula, Mljet and Dubrovnik.

Dalmatian Coast Map on p74

Brela (p82) ANNA LURYE/SHUTTERSTOCK ©

Top Sights 📷
Ston Walls

The economic importance of the salt industry to the Republic of Ragusa (Dubrovnik) led, in 1333, to the construction of one of the longest fortifications in Europe, stretching clear across the isthmus that connects the Pelješac Peninsula with the mainland. Twenty towers and 5.5km of this extraordinary wall are still standing, arching far up the hill between the town of Ston and its diminutive sibling Mali ('little') Ston.

◎ MAP P74, E4

Stonske zidine

adult/child 70/30KN

⏱8am-6.30pm Apr-Oct, 9am-3pm Nov-Mar

Walking the Walls

Famous architects, including Juraj Dalmatinac (best known for Šibenik Cathedral), were involved in the design and construction of Ston's extraordinary 14th-century defenses, which originally included 40 towers and five forts, and stretched for 7km. You can walk the Ston section in 15 minutes; allow an extra 30 sweaty minutes to continue up and over the hill to Mali Ston. Admission includes entry to the substantially reconstructed Fort St Jerome (Tvrđava sv Jeronima), a square castle with a tower at each corner positioned on Ston's southeastern flank.

Ston

Within its walls, Ston has an atmospheric medieval town centre with sunny, car-less streets and some good restaurants. The name Ston derives from its Latin name Stagnum, a reference to the marshy nature of the land, which the Romans put to use for the production of salt. The salt pans at **Solana Ston** (☏020-754 027; www.solanaston.hr; Pelješki put 1; with/without guide 25/15KN; ☉7am-8pm) have operated in much the same way for over 700 years. An introductory video explains the process, after which you can take a walk around the evaporation pans and the factory building.

Mali Ston

The fishing village of Mali Ston is a gastronomic destination in its own right, famed for the mussels and large flat oysters (harvested here since Roman times) which thrive in the narrow channel separating the peninsula from the mainland.

Prapatno

The closest beach to Ston, this gem of a bay has a sandy shore and clear, calm waters, making it a hit with local families. It's 4km southwest of Ston, near the ferry to Mljet.

★ Top Tips

o Salt is gathered at Solana Ston between late July and September and volunteers are needed to help out – it's a kind of working holiday; see www.solanaston. hr for info.

o In summer, you can usually buy a bag of salt from a stand set up at the gate.

✕ Take a Break

Kapetanova Kuća
(☏020-754 264; www. ostrea.hr; Mali Ston; mains 95-140KN; ☉9am-midnight) is one of the most venerable seafood restaurants in the region. Feast on Ston oysters and grilled squid on the shady terrace, but try to leave room for the Stonski makaruli, a macaroni cake that's a local specialty.

On the Ston side, grab a seat in the lovely garden courtyard at **Stagnum** (☏020-754 158; Imena Isusova 23; mains 35-130KN; ☉11am-midnight May-Sep).

Dalmatian Coast

For reviews see	
◉ Top Sights	p72
⊙ Sights	p75

BOSNIA &
HERZEGOVINA

● Nevesinje

● Stolac

Mostar ●

● Široki
Brijeg

● Čitluk

● Međugorje

● Čapljina

Neretva

Metković ●

● Vid

Neum ●

Ston Walls
D8

Slano ●

● Polače

Mljetski Channel

Pomena ●
● Polače

Mljet
National
Park

Sobra ●

Mljet ●

Šipan ●

Šipanska Luka

Trsteno

Zaton

Sudurad ●

● Luka

Dubrovnik

Elafiti Islands ●

● Posušje

● Imotski

60

● Trilj

E65

● Zagvozd

Biokovo Nature Park ⊙
▲ Sv Jure (1762m)

● Vrgorac

● Drvenik

D8
Ploče ●

Mala
Sea

● Janjina

Pelješac Peninsula

Neretvanski
Channel

Trpanj ●

Orebić ● ②

Viganj

③

Korčula Town ●

Lumbarda ●

● Korčula

Korčulanski
Channel

● Blato

Vela Luka ●

● Proizd

Lastovski Channel

Pasadur ●

● Lastovo

Lastovo ●

● Ubli

● Podgora

Igrane ●

Sućuraj ●

Makarska ⑤ ⊙
Tučepić ●
Selca ⑥
Baška Voda ⑦
Brela ●
Pučišća ●
D8
Zagvozd ●

Sumartin ●

● Vrboska

Jelsa ●

Zavala ●

● Šćedro

▲
(626m)
Sv Nikola

Trogir ●
Čiovo ●

Drvenik
Veli ●

Maslinica ●

Split

Kaštela ●

Klis ●

Solin ⑨

V Kabal
(339m)

E65

T

● Podstrana & Stobreč ⑧

Omiš ●

Dugi Rat ●

Splitski
Channel

● Rogač

Supetar ●

Postira ●

● Brač

Milna ●

Brački Channel

▲ Vidova Gora
(778m)

Bol ●

Hvarski Channel

Stari Grad ●

● Hvar

Hvar

Pakleni
Islands

Viški
Channel

Rukavac ●

Vis Town ●

● Vis

Komiža ●

Biševo ●

● Primošten

Rogoznica ●

D8

Drvenik
Mali ●

Šolta ●

Stomorska ●

Susac ●

Adriatic Sea

0 ——— 20 km
0 ——— 10 miles

N

E

F

1

2

3

4

A B C D

Trsteno

1  MAP P74, F4

Lovers of gardens (and *Game of Thrones*) shouldn't miss this small coastal settlement, only 19km from Dubrovnik's old town. It was during the Renaissance that Dubrovnik's nobles started to pay extra attention to their gardens. Ivan Gučetić started the trend at his Trsteno estate in 1494, and his descendants maintained the garden throughout the centuries. The land was eventually taken over by the Yugoslav Academy of Sciences & Arts, which turned it into the public **Trsteno Arboretum** (☎020-751 019; adult/child 50/30KN; ⊙7am-7pm May-Oct, 8am-4pm Nov-Apr). *Game of Thrones* fans will recognise it as the location

used for the Red Keep gardens, where the Tyrells chatted and plotted endlessly during seasons three and four.

The garden has a Renaissance layout, with a set of geometric shapes formed with plants such as lavender, rosemary, fuchsia and bougainvillea, while citrus trees perfume the air. It's set around a stone villa (built around 1500), with a cliff-edge pavilion in front and a chapel behind. There's also a small hedge maze, a fine palm collection (including Chinese windmill palms) and a gorgeous pond overlooked by a statue of Neptune and filled with white waterlilies and dozens of bullfrogs and goldfish. It's only partially landscaped, though – quite a bit of it is wonderfully wild.

Dalmatian Coast Trsteno

Trsteno Arboretum

Pelješac Wine Trail

As they zip along the winding road through the centre of the Pelješac Peninsula, travellers may not be aware that they're passing through the realm of the king of Croatian red wines: *plavac mali*.

A descendant of *crljenak kaštelanski* (more commonly known as *zinfandel* or *primitivo*) and little-known *dobričić*, this little *(mali)* blue *(plavac)* grape produces big, flavoursome wine. The more inhospitable the terrain, the more flavour-laden the grapes, which is why the very best *plavac mali* is grown on the barren, sun-baked slopes of **Dingač** and **Postup** on the peninsula's southern coast. The vines are so difficult to access that all of the grapes must be harvested by hand. Both of these regions are now recognised appellations, protected by a 'stamp of geographic origin'.

You couldn't hope for a more authentically rustic spot to sample a local drop than **Taverna Domanoeta** (☏ 091 56 01 591; ⏰ 9am-1am Jul & Aug), a stone-walled cellar bar in **Janjina**, a small village at the very centre of the peninsula. If it's sunny, grab a table in the garden and order some *plavac mali*, accompanied by local cheese and *pršut* (prosciutto).

A little further on is the turn-off for the village of **Trstenik**, where legendary Napa Valley winemaker Mike Grgich has established **Grgić Vina** (☏ 020-748 090; www.grgic-vina.com; Trstenik 78; tasting 40KN; ⏰ 9am-9pm Jun-Aug, to 5pm Mon-Fri Sep-May). Call in to the winery to buy the award-winning *plavac mali* and *pošip* (a white varietal that originated on Korčula); phone ahead in winter.

The main road continues through a valley to **Potomje** village, where a 400m tunnel cuts through the mountain to the famed winegrowing slopes of Dingač. Of the many wineries in Potomje, the best to visit is **Matuško** (☏ 020-742 393; www.matusko-vina.hr; Potomje 5a; ⏰ 8am-8pm Mar-Dec), where you can check out the extensive cellars before sitting down to a free tasting.

If all this wine tasting is making you thirsty, stop at **Peninsula** (☏ 020-742 503; www.peninsula.hr; ⏰ 9am-11pm Apr-Oct; 🛜), a roadside wine bar with over 40 high-quality local wines, as well as a selection of *rakija* (grappa) and liqueurs. It's located in **Donja Banda**, near where the road from Trpanj branches off from the main peninsula road.

Look out for the two giant plane trees at the entrance to the village – each is more than 500 years old and around 50m high. They're among the largest of their kind in Europe.

Orebić

2 🎯 **MAP P74, D3**

Orebić (population 1980), on the southern coast of the Pelješac Peninsula, has a strip of lovely little beaches, some sandy and some shingly, bordered by groves of tamarisk and pine. Its waterfront is lined with houses and exotic gardens built by the sea captains who made the town prosperous in the 18th century. Only 2.5km across the water from Korčula Town, it makes a perfect day trip or an alternative base.

The Pelješac Peninsula became part of Dubrovnik in 1333 when it was purchased from Serbia. The name Orebić comes from a wealthy seafaring family who, in 1658, built a citadel as a defence against the Turks. The height of Orebić seafaring was in the 18th and 19th centuries when it was the seat of one of the largest companies of the day: the Associazione Marittima di Sabbioncello. This history is recalled in the town's moderately interesting **Maritime Museum** (Pomorski muzej; 🖊020-713 009; Trg Mimbeli bb; adult/child 15/10KN; ⊗7am-8pm Mon-Fri, 4-8pm Sat & Sun Jun-Oct, 7am-3pm Mon-Fri Nov-May). It contains model ships, maritime paintings, boating memorabilia, navigational aids and Roman ceramics sourced from shipwrecks, but few captions are in English.

There's a slim beach west of the dock, but the best beach is the long stretch at **Trstenica** about 700m east of the dock, a beautiful long crescent of sand and fine shingle fringed by mature trees.

Orebić is great base for hiking, so pick up a trail map from the **tourist office** (🖊020-713 718; www.visitorebic-croatia.hr; Zrinsko Frankopanska 2; ⊗8am-10pm Jul & Aug, to 8pm Mon-Sat May, Jun, Sep & Oct, to 1pm Mon-Fri Nov-Apr). A track through the pine trees leads from the Hotel Bellevue to a 15th-century **Franciscan monastery** on a ridge 152m above the sea. From this vantage point, Dubrovnik patrols could watch the Venetian ships moored on Korčula and notify the authorities of any suspicious movements. The village of **Karmen**, near the monastery, is the starting point for walks to picturesque upper villages and the more daring climb up **Mt Ilija**, the bare, grey massif that hangs over Orebić. The reward for climbers is a sweeping view of the entire coast. On a hill east of the monastery is **Our-Lady-of-Carmel Church**, next to several huge cypresses, as well as a baroque loggia and the ruins of a duke's castle.

Call ahead to arrange a visit to **Korta Katarina** (🖊020-713 817; www.kortakatarinawinery.com; Bana Josipa Jelačića 3; ⊗9am-9pm May-Sep, to 4pm Apr & Oct). This large, schmick winery offers a standard tour including tastings of three wines (100KN), VIP tastings with an extra reserve wine and snacks

Neum Corridor

Due to a historical anomaly, the coastal highway passes through 9km of Bosnian territory immediately north of the Pelješac Peninsula. You'll need to have your passports handy for the two sets of border crossings, and drivers may need to produce their car's third-party-insurance green slip. Check in advance with your car-hire company if you're considering taking this route, as some charge an additional fee.

To bypass Bosnia completely, head along the Pelješac Peninsula to Trpanj and catch the car ferry to Ploče (passenger/car 32/138KN, four to seven daily); it usually cuts around 30 minutes off the trip.

If you're wondering how this unusual situation came about, it dates from the time when Dubrovnik was a republic and Venice controlled the remainder of the Dalmatian Coast. The wily southerners made a deal with the Ottoman Turks (who ruled neighbouring Bosnia), giving them a land corridor to the Adriatic and, in the process, gaining a buffer between their republic and the Venetians.

After WWI and the demise of the Ottoman Empire, the borders disappeared within the newly established Yugoslavia. It wasn't until the 1990s war that they reappeared, leaving Dubrovnik without a land connection to the rest of Croatia. A bridge is currently being built to link the two parts of the country. However this project is controversial as it will pass over Bosnia's territorial waters.

(300KN), and gastro tastings include a five-course meal with wine matches (700KN).

Satisfy a sweet urge with a strudel, a slice of cake or a homemade gelato at chilled-out little **Croccantino cafe** (☎098 16 50 777; www.facebook.com/CroccantinoCRO; Obala Pomoraca 30; snacks 8-18KN; ☺7am-11pm) on the promenade.

A bright mural of a city street provides a cheerfully anachronistic backdrop for breezy restaurant **Konoba Andiamo** (☎098 98 38 614; Šetalište kneza Domagoja 28; mains 50-120KN; ☺1pm-midnight Jun-Oct; ☞), set in a wooden terrace just metres from the sea. We wholeheartedly endorse the seafood platter for two, packed with prawns, mussels, langoustine and two types of fish. With advance notice they'll also roast lamb, pork, veal or octopus under a *peka* (charcoal-covered metal dome).

La Casa (☎020-713 847; Obala Pomoraca 40; mains 43-145KN; ☺noon-10pm; ☞) has a funky garden bar downstairs, but head up to the terrace of this grand old house for sea views and tasty

Neapolitan-style pizza. They also serve pasta, risotto, steaks and grilled squid.

Jadrolinija car ferries from Korčula (passenger/car 16/76KN, 15 minutes) tie up just steps from the tourist office and bus stop. Buses head to/from Ston (51KN, 1½ hours, three daily), Dubrovnik (81KN, 2¾ hours, two daily) and Split (121KN, 4½ hours, daily).

Viganj

3 MAP P74, C3

If you're into windsurfing or kite-surfing, Viganj (population 280) has some of the best conditions in Croatia. The village is strung out along the coast 7km west of Orebić, near the tip of the Pelješac

Peninsula. It's a sluggish place in the off-season, but in summer there are a couple of restaurants, a lively beach bar and a little **tourist office** (☎020-719 059; www.visitorebic-croatia.hr; ⏰9am-2pm Mon-Sat mid-Jun–mid-Sep). There's no public transport to Viganj; the narrow coastal road is extremely slow going in summer.

Vid

4 MAP P74, E3

Huddled on a hill by the sleepy Norin River, tiny Vid (population 796) stands out amid the lush green flatlands of the Neretva River valley. Once a thriving Roman settlement named Narona and later ruled by the Neretva

Harbour at Orebić (p77)

pirates, today it is one of the only parts of southern Dalmatia where the economy relies on agriculture rather than tourism.

In 1995 archaeologists in Vid made the extraordinary discovery of an Augusteum, a temple dedicated to the cult of the Roman Emperors, built around 10 BC. Along with a simple monochromatic floor mosaic they found 17 marble statues of the Imperial family, all of which had been decapitated when the temple was destroyed in the 4th century. Two of the statues (those of Augustus' wife Livia and the later emperor Vespasian) have been reunited with their heads, one of which had been exhibited in Oxford's Ashmolean Museum since its discovery in 1878. The site is now enclosed within the **Narona Archaeological Museum** (Arheološki muzej Narona; 020-691 596; www.a-m-narona.hr; Naronski trg 6; adult/student 40/20KN; 9am-7pm Tue-Sun Jun-Sep, to 4pm Tue-Sat, to 1pm Sun Oct-May), an impressive piece of contemporary architecture showcasing the temple and other exhibits highlighting the area's history. You can also climb up to the rooftop for splendid vistas.

Established by two best friends a quarter of a century ago, **Đuđa i Mate** (020-687 500; www.djudjaimate.hr; Velika Riva 2; mains 60-100KN; 9am-11pm) is a restaurant famous for its Neretva regional specialties, particularly frogs and eels. Try them fried, grilled or combined in a Neretva brudet – a flavourful spiced stew served with polenta. They also offer 45-minute 'safaris' along the Norin River in a shallow, traditional boat called a trupa.

To get to Vid from the coastal highway, follow the signs onto the E73 to Metković. In Metković, turn left onto the bridge across the Neretva River and follow the signs. There are no regular buses to Vid but many intercity services stop in Metković, 3.5km away, from where you can continue by cab.

Biokovo Nature Park

5 **MAP P74, D2**

The hulking limestone Biokovo massif offers hiking opportunities with views aplenty. You can also drive on a rough, single-track, 23km road all the way to Sveti Jure (1762m), its highest peak. Park entry fees apply, payable at the **Biokovo Nature Park booth** (Park Prirode Biokovo; www.biokovo.com; adult/child 50/25KN; 7am-8pm mid-May–Sep, 8am-4pm Apr–mid-May & Oct–mid-Nov) at the beginning of Biokovska, the main road that runs up the mountain, accessed from the Makarska–Vrgorac highway.

Just up from the village of the same name, the **Kotišina Botanical Garden** (Botanički vrt Kotišina; admission free) is a wild, 16.5-hectare expanse of mountainside filled with well-labelled indigenous flora. Ranging in height from 350m to 500m above sea level, the site

Tasty Tučepi

If you have a car, there are a couple of great options in the hills above the village of Tučepi, southeast of Makarska.

Jeny Restaurant (☎ 091 58 78 078; www.restaurant-jeny.hr; Čovići 1, Gornji Tučepi; menu with/without wine 780/600KN; ⏱ 6pm–midnight mid-May–Sep; ⚲) In this fine-dining restaurant on the slopes of Biokovo mountain, the culinary focus is Mediterranean with a French touch. There's no *a la carte* option, only a seven-course *degustation*, which can be tailored for vegetarians or those with allergies (let them know when you book). The breathtaking riviera views make up for the passable decor.

Konoba Ranč (☎ 021-623 563; www.ranc-tucepi.hr; Kamena 62, Tučepi; mains 90-200KN; ⏱ 6pm-1am Apr-Sep) This rustic spot, away from the tourist buzz, is worth the 10-minute drive from Makarska; follow the sign leading up from the highway. Dine on log chairs under olive trees, feasting on grilled meat and fish, a preordered meat or seafood *peka*, house wine and sporadic *klapa* (traditional singing) performances.

offers spectacular views over the islands of Brač and Hvar. Rocky paths lead past a fort built into a cave and up a canyon. Good shoes are a must.

Makarska

6 ◉ MAP P74, C2

Makarska (population 13,900) is a beach resort with a spectacular natural setting, backed by the glorious Biokovo mountain range. While the outskirts are a little shabby, there's a lovely long waterfront promenade and a pretty limestone centre that turns peachy orange at sunset. Active types base themselves here to take advantage of the nearby hiking, climbing, paragliding, mountain-biking, windsurfing and swimming opportunities, and the good transport connections.

The high season is pretty raucous, with many buzzing nightlife spots, but it's also a lot of fun for those with children. If you're interested in hanging around beach bars and clubs, playing volleyball and generally lounging about, you'll like Makarska. Outside the high season, things are quiet.

Makarska's harbour and historic centre are located on a large cove bordered by Cape Osejava in the southeast and the Sveti Petar peninsula in the northwest. The long pebble **town beach**, lined with hotels, stretches from the Sveti Petar park northwest along the bay. For a party atmosphere, head past the town beach to **Buba beach**, near the Hotel Rivijera, where music pumps all day during summer. To the southeast are rockier and lovelier beaches, such as **Nugal**, popular with nudists.

Kill time on a rainy day tracing the town's history in the **Makarska Municipal Museum** (Gradski muzej Makarska; ☎021-612 302; Obala kralja Tomislava 17; 10KN; ☺9am-1pm Mon-Sat), or head to the **Franciscan Monastery** (Franjevački samostan & Malakološki muzej; ☎099 88 52 165; Franjevački 1; museum 15KN; ☺museum 10am-noon May-Sep, by arrangement Oct-Apr) where there's a huge contemporary mosaic in the apse of the church and a well-presented shell museum tucked around the back (enter from Alkarska), the labour of love of a past friar.

The best place for traditional food is **Konoba Kalalarga** (Kalalarga 40; mains from 50KN; ☺9am-2am Tue-Sun; ☎), a tavern with dim lighting, dark wood and alfresco bench seating in an alleyway leading up from Makarska's main square. There's no menu – the waiter will run through the specials.

The **Grabovac wine bar** (Kačićev trg 11; ☺9am-2am Apr-Oct; ☎), by the church on the main square, is an outpost of a famous winery from Imotski (the wine region directly behind the mountains, right on the Bosnian border). It serves its own wine by the glass, plus tasty titbits such as local cheese and *pršut*.

Occupying a sea cave near the Hotel Osejava, **Deep** (www.facebook.com/deepmakarska; Šetalište dr fra Jure Radića 5a; ☺9am-5am Jun–mid-Sep; ☎) attracts a fashionable set who sip cocktails as a DJ spins the latest beats. Cover charges kick in after 11pm.

Makarska is a major transport hub, with car ferries to Sumartin on Brač (passenger/car 30/150KN, one hour); seasonal catamarans to Dubrovnik (160KN, 3¼ hours), Sobra on Mljet (140KN, 2¼ hours), Korčula Town (130KN, one hour), Bol on Brač (90KN, 35 minutes) and Split (100KN, 1½ hours); and buses to Dubrovnik (105KN, three hours, eight daily) and Split (50KN, 1¼ hours, at least hourly).

Brela

7 ◉ MAP P74, C2

The longest and arguably the loveliest coastline in Dalmatia stretches through the holiday town of Brela (population 1710). Six kilometres of pebble beaches curve around coves thickly forested with pine trees, where you can enjoy beautifully clear seas and fantastic sunsets. A shady promenade lined with bars and cafes winds around the coves, which spread out on both sides of the town. The best beach is **Punta Rata**, a gorgeous spit of pebbles and pines about 300m northwest of the town centre.

If you're after a treat, take a 20-minute walk to **Del Posto** (☏021-604 890; Obala Sv Nikole 71, Baška Voda; mains 50-90KN; ⏰7am-11pm; 🛜), an elegant restaurant and wine bar on the terrace of the flashy Grand Hotel Slavia in **Baška Voda**, the next town along the coast. The prices are surprisingly reasonable for the somewhat rarefied ambience, and the grilled squid is excellent.

Most buses running along the highway stop near the Brela turn-off, 1km above the town centre. Destinations include Split (35KN, one hour, hourly), Makarska (18KN, 20 minutes, hourly) and Dubrovnik (110KN, 3½ hours, four daily). Free parking is hard to come by, even in the low season.

Omiš

8 ◉ **MAP P74, B1**

The legendary pirates' lair of Omiš (population 15,000) has one of the most dramatic locations of any town on the Dalmatian coast. Situated at the mouth of the Cetina River, at the end of a picturesque canyon, it's backed by sheer walls of mottled grey rock topped with craggy peaks.

The coastal-highway traffic slows to a crawl as the road narrows into the leafy oak-lined main street. On the landward side is a small but atmospheric maze of old lanes capped with a little castle. A sandy-shingly beach stretches out on its other flank, attracting scores of families in summer.

Dalmatian Coast Omiš

Biokova Nature Park (p80)

Abutting a sunny square at the centre of the old town, early-17th-century **St Michael's Church** (Župna crkva sv Mihovila; Trg Sv Mihovila; ⏰ hours vary) has an ornate entrance carved from Brač stone, including Corinthian columns decorated in an interesting fish-scale pattern. Inside there's a single nave with a high vaulted ceiling, a gilded high altar and some beautiful paintings.

Mirabela Fortress (Tvrđava Mirabela; 20KN; ⏰ 9am-9pm May-Oct), also known as Peovica, was built in the 13th century on 9th-century Byzantine foundations. It's reached by a steep set of steps, and while there's not a lot inside, it's worth trudging up the internal staircase and taking the final ladder to the top for the views over the town.

Omiš' enviable location lends itself to plenty of activities. The most gentle option is a cruise up the river canyon to pretty **Radmanove Mlinice** (Radman's Mills; around 100KN); small boats line up alongside the bridge and depart when full. More adventurous types can blast along the **zipline** (📱 095 82 22 221; www.zipline-croatia.com; Josipa Pupačića 4; 400KN) strung high above the Cetina canyon – up to 150m high, to be exact. The longest of the eight wires runs for 700m; the price includes transfers from Omiš.

Rafting is possible upstream from Omiš from spring to autumn, but the rapids can become quite fast after heavy rains. Summer is best for inexperienced rafters. Operators tout their trips from the riverside; the better ones charge upwards of 200KN.

Operating out of an old stone house right on the traffic-choked main street, **Bastion** (📱 021-757 922; Fošal 9; mains 59-195KN; ⏰ 10am-midnight; 📶) serves a tasty selection of grilled meat as well as pizza and lots of seafood. Try the black risotto or call ahead for an octopus to be chucked under the *peka*.

Omiš' hippest eatery, **La Fabbrica** (📱 091 89 00 212; www.facebook.com/lafabbricaomis; Fošal 19; mains 50-120KN; ⏰ 9am-midnight Sun-Thu, to 2am Fri & Sat; 📶) serves the likes of burgers and steaks alongside such traditional dishes as *pašticada* (a rich meaty stew), pasta and grilled fish, and more adventurous fare like truffle cappuccino soup. The vibe is relaxed and bar-like, and there's regular live music in summer.

There are lots of bars on the little squares within the old town's cobbled core. At weekends it gets surprisingly lively – despite the tiny size of most venues. **Turjun** (Fošal 9; ⏰ 7am-2am May-Sep, to 10pm Oct-Apr; 📶) inhabits a tower which is all that remains of the historic town gate. Omiš' more bohemian types gravitate to wee **Lix** (Ivana Katušića 5; ⏰ 9am-midnight) and hold court at the scattering of tables on the marbled lane or inside the stone-walled interior.

Split city bus 60 heads here every half-hour (22KN). Coach destinations include Makarska (32KN, 45 minutes, hourly) and Dubrovnik (121KN, four hours, four daily).

Podstrana & Stobreč

9 ◉ MAP P74, B1

Positioned under the mountains at the foot of the Split peninsula, these neighbouring settlements sit on opposite sides of a sheltered bay, divided by the Žrnovnica River. Podstrana has the disadvantage of the coastal highway passing right through it, but it has some nice beaches and a flash resort hotel. Stobreč is the prettier of the two, with a marina and partly sandy beach. It started life in the 3rd century BC as the Greek town of Epetion.

Stobreč has a couple of noteworthy eateries, including a well-known seafood restaurant. Grilled meat takes centre stage at friendly family-run **Kaša Grill & Bar** (☎021-325 083; www.facebook.com/kasagrillbar; Alojzija Stepinca 17, Stobreč; mains 50-120KN; ◷noon-3pm & 6pm-midnight; 🛜), tucked away on a residential street set back from the water. Local oddities such as steak stuffed with cheese and prosciutto sit alongside the likes of lamb chops, veal livers, chicken fillets and burgers.

Omiš (p83)

Worth a Trip 🔭
Mljet National Park

Covering 5400 hectares of land and sea at the western end of the island of Mljet, this national park offers shady walking and cycling tracks, a ruggedly beautiful coastline, ancient ruins and saltwater lakes. The main hubs are the villages of Pomena and Polače, which buzz with visitors on summer days but quieten down again once all the boats leave.

Nacionalni park Mljet

☎ 020-744 041

www.np-mljet.hr

Pristanište 2

adult/child Jun-Sep 125/70KN, Oct-May 70/50K

⏱ office 8am-8pm Apr-Oct

Saltwater Lakes

The centrepieces of the national park are forest-fringed **Malo Jezero** (Little Lake) and **Veliko Jezero** (Big Lake), a pair of saltwater lakes connected to each other by a short channel. The larger lake then empties into the sea via the much longer **Soline Canal**, which makes the lakes subject to tidal flows.

The monks from nearby Sveta Marija Island deepened and widened the channel between the lakes, building a mill to take advantage of the rush of sea water as the tide rose and fell. The mill is long gone and the channel is now spanned by a bridge.

The area around **Mali Most** (Little Bridge) is the busiest swimming spot in the national park. It's a lovely place for a dip, but we suggest that you stroll along the shore of Malo Jezero until you find a quiet nook of your own.

You can walk completely around the little lake but not the big one, as there's no bridge over the Soline Channel. If you decide to swim it, keep in mind that the current can be strong.

Sveta Marija Island

Tiny **St Mary's Island** lies on Veliko Jezero, not far from its southern shore. Boats (included in the park admission price) head here at least hourly during park opening hours, departing from Mali Most and from Pristanište on the lake's northern shore.

The island's **Benedictine monastery** was founded in 1198 but has been rebuilt several times, adding Renaissance and baroque features to the Romanesque structure. The Benedictine order effectively ruled the entire island of Mljet from the 13th century until it was formally annexed by the Republic of Ragusa (Dubrovnik) in 1410.

The monastery continued to operate until 1809, when it was closed by the French

★ Top Tips

○ Kiosks in Pomena and Polače sell park admission tickets, which include the boat ride to Sveta Marija.

○ From Polače, your ticket includes a transfer to the main park information centre at Pristanište on Veliko Jezero.

○ From Pomena, it's a 400m walk along a forested path to Malo Jezero.

✗ Take a Break

Konoba Galija (☏ 095 91 12 588; Pomena 7a; mains 80-220KN; ☼ noon-11pm) is one of a string of seafood restaurants on the Pomena waterfront, each with its own yacht moorings and seawater tank.

★ Getting There

Car A car ferry heads between Prapratno and Sobra, 26km east of Polače. It's possible to hire cars and scooters at Sobra.
Catamaran Seasonal ferries head to Pomena and Polače.

administration following the Napoleonic conquest. It housed state offices up until 1960 when it was converted into a hotel, which closed in 1991 during the war. It has since been returned to the Catholic church, which is in the process of restoring it.

The complex includes the large St Mary's Church, a couple of tiny chapels, stables with a resident donkey, and the monks' former living quarters, which now has a restaurant in its basement. There are also ruins of a Roman building in the island's centre.

You can explore the entire island in less than an hour, but many people choose to linger for a swim or a glass of wine on the terrace of the restaurant.

Polače

The fishing village of Polače is less glitzy than its neighbour, Pomena, with a more lived-in feel despite the seasonal tourist influx. Its blissful position on a sheltered inlet on the northern edge of the island has made it a desirable location since ancient times.

At the time of the Roman conquest in 35 BC, the island was populated by the Illyrians, who erected hill forts and traded with the mainland. The Romans expanded the settlement around Polače, eventually building a palace complete with baths and servants' quarters.

It's hard to miss the high, hulking walls of the **Roman Palace** (Rimska palača) on the Polače waterfront; the structure is so large that the road was built right through the

Sveta Marija Island (p87)

centre of it. Constructed around the 5th century, this massive residential complex has a rectangular floor plan, with high defensive towers on the front corners separated by a pier. Other ancient ruins scattered around the town include a Late Antiquity fort and an early Christian church.

There's a nice little swimming spot near the palace, and the village has cafes, a **tourist office** (☏ 020-744 186; www.mljet.hr; ⏰ 9am-1pm & 4-7pm Mon-Sat, 9am-1pm Sun Jun-Sep, 8am-1pm Mon-Fri Oct-May) and agencies renting cars, scooters, bikes and kayaks.

Walking & Cycling

The name Mljet comes from the Ancient Greek word 'Melita', meaning 'honey', a reference to the many bees humming in the forests. The island is still covered in lush foliage, and visitors can delve into it via the network of walking and cycling paths heading through the national park. Enquire about routes at the main park office in Pristanište or at the tourist office in Polače.

Bikes are available to rent from various locations in Pomena and Polače for around 20KN per hour. Cycling is an excellent way to explore but be aware that the two villages are separated by a steep hill. The lakeside bike path is an easier pedal and very scenic.

Mljet vs Malta

Mljet shares the same Ancient Greek name as the island nation of Malta, deriving from their word for honey. This has led both islands to claim themselves as the site for St Paul's shipwreck, as described in the Acts of the Apostles in the Bible. Most editions translate the original Greek text to Malta, but Mljet's claim is bolstered by a reference to the island being in the Adriatic Sea.

Diving

Mljet offers some interesting diving opportunities, including a German WWII torpedo boat and several walls. There's also a 3rd-century Roman wreck in relatively shallow water. The remains of the ship, including amphorae, have calcified over the centuries and this has protected them from pillaging. **Aquatica** (☏ 098 479 916; www.aquatica-mljet.hr), based in Pomena, offers boat dives and diving courses.

Saplunara

It's well worth venturing outside the national park to explore the rest of Mljet. Saplunara, at the opposite end of the island, has beautiful beaches, good accommodation and an excellent restaurant.

Explore 🧭
Korčula Town & Korčula Island

Rich in vineyards, olive groves and small villages, and harbouring a glorious old town, the island of Korčula is the sixth-largest Adriatic island, stretching nearly 47km in length. Korčula Town is breathtaking. Ringed by imposing defences, this coastal citadel is dripping with history, its marble streets lined with Renaissance and Gothic buildings.

Start by wandering through Korčula's old town, stopping to explore St Mark's Cathedral (p92) and the Korčula Town Museum (p95). If you're interested in religious art, call in to the Icon Museum (p95) and Abbey Treasury (p93). Take a drive to Konoba Mate (p98) for lunch. Afterwards, head down the steep hill to Pupnatska Luka for a swim before returning to Korčula Town in time for a sunset cocktail at Massimo (p99).

Getting There & Around

🚌 Routes connecting Ston, Dubrovnik and Split to Korčula Town use the Orebić car ferry.

⚓ Car ferries head between Orebić and Dominče, 3km east of Korčula Town, and between Split and Vela Luka. Catamarans head to Korčula Town's West Harbour from Hvar and Split year-round, with seasonal services from Dubrovnik, Mljet, Makarska and Bol.

Korčula Town Map on p94

Korčula Town TUUL & BRUNO MORANDI/GETTY IMAGES ©

Top Sights 📷
St Mark's Cathedral

Dominating the little square at Korčula's heart is this magnificent 15th-century cathedral, built from Korčula limestone in a Gothic-Renaissance style by Italian and local artisans. The sculptural detail of the facade is intriguing, particularly the naked squatting figures of Adam and Eve on the door pillars, and the two-tailed mermaid and elephant on the triangular gable cornice at the top.

◎ MAP P94, C3

Katedrala svetog Marka

Trg Sv Marka

church 10KN, bell tower adult/child 20/15KN

🕑 9am-9pm Jul & Aug, hours vary Sep-Jun

Interior

Inside, the nave soars 30m in height and is lined with a twin colonnade of limestone pillars. Look out for the *ciborium* (altar canopy), carved by Korčulan Marko Andrijić, and behind it the altarpiece painting *Three Saints*, by Tintoretto. Another painting attributed to Tintoretto or his workshop, *The Annunciation*, is beside the altar of St Anthony.

Other noteworthy artworks include a bronze statue of St Blaise by Ivan Meštrović near the altar on the northern aisle, and a painting by the Venetian artist Jacopo Bassano in the apse of the southern aisle. Check out the modern sculptures in the baptistery too.

Bell Tower

The bell tower is topped by a balustrade and ornate cupola, also beautifully carved by Andrijić.

St Mark's Abbey Treasury

The 14th-century **Abbey Palace** (Opatska riznica svetog Marka; incl cathedral 25KN; ☉9am-7pm Mon-Sat May-Nov) houses an important collection of icons and Dalmatian religious art. The most outstanding work is the 1431 polyptych of *The Virgin & Child with Saints* by Blaž Jurjev of Trogir. The 20th century is represented by a sketch by Ivan Meštrović and a painting by Đuro Pulitika. There are also liturgical items, jewellery, coins, furniture and ancient documents relating to the history of Korčula.

Holy Week

Beginning on Palm Sunday, the entire week before Easter is devoted to ceremonies and processions organised by the local religious brotherhoods dressed in traditional costumes. The most solemn processions are on Good Friday evening when members of all brotherhoods parade through the streets.

★ **Top Tips**

○ Outside of July and August the cathedral's opening hours vary widely. You'll find it open around Mass times and religious feasts (especially Holy Week), and when large tour groups are in town.

○ The bell tower is only open at busy times. Climb to the top for views over the old town.

○ Before leaving the square, stop to admire the elegantly ornamented Arneri Palace opposite the cathedral, at the corner of the narrow street of the same name.

✕ **Take a Break**

Korčula Town's best restaurants are all a short walk from the the cathedral. Our top picks are Marco's (p97) and LD Terrace (p97); the latter has the added bonus of sea views.

A **B** **C** **D**

Korčula Island

Korčulanski Channel

See Main Map

Pelješac Peninsula

Mt Ilija (961m)

Viganj

Orebić

Zeča (565m)

Pupnat

Korčula Town

Vela Luka

Žrnovo

Blato

Smokvica

Pupnatska Luka

Lumbarda

Pržina

Adriatic Sea

Lastovski Channel

1

2

Pelješki Channel

9

Sv Barbare

Antuna Rozanovića

Sv Roka

Korčulanskih Bratovština

Pomenića

Španić

Don Luke Depola

Dr Vinka Foretića

Trg Sv Marka

Biskupa Luke Tolentića Depolo

3

Obala dr Franje Tuđmana

Rafa Arneri

Dr Dinka Miroševića

St Mark's Cathedral

Don Pavla Poše

Kalafata

Ismaelli

1 **Korčula Town Museum**

Biskupije

6

West Harbour

Giunio

OLD TOWN

Marka Andrijića

4

Trg Korčulanskih klesara i kipara

Od Teatra

Baničevića

7

Žlinica

Korčulanskog Statuta

Don Iva Matijace

Šetalište Petra Kanavelića

5

Kaporova

2

Icon Museum

Trg Braće Radić

10

Dobrotvornosti

3

Veliki Revelin Tower

Foša

Foša

5

Put Sv Nikole

Trg Pomirenja

Trg Kralja Tomislava

11

Plokata 19 Travnja 1921

Trg Sv Justine

Prolaz

6

4

Punta Jurana

8

Hrvatske Bratske Zajednice

Bus Station (75m)

Tri Sulara

N 0 ————— 100 m

For reviews see	
◉	Top Sights	p92
◎	Sights	p95
✪	Eating	p96
✪	Drinking	p98
✪	Entertainment	p99
🏠	Shopping	p99

A **B** **C** **D**

Sights

Korčula Town Museum MUSEUM

1 ◎ MAP P94, C4

Occupying the 16th-century Gabriellis Palace, this museum traces the history and culture of Korčula throughout the ages. Displays cover stonemasonry, shipbuilding, archaeology, art, furniture, textiles and examples of Korčulan traditional dress. There are some interesting curios scattered over its four floors – including a tablet recording the Greek presence on the island in the 3rd century BC. (Gradski muzej Korčula; ☑020-711 420; www.gm-korcula.com; Trg Sv Marka 20; adult/child 20/8KN; ⊙9am-9pm Jul-Sep, 10am-1pm Oct-Jun)

Icon Museum MUSEUM

2 ◎ MAP P94, D4

This modest museum has a collection of interesting Byzantine icons, painted on gilded wood, and 17th- and 18th-century ritual objects. The real highlight is access to gorgeous 15th-century **All Saints' Church** (Crkva Svih Svetih) next door. This baroque church features a 17th-century painted Cretan crucifix, an extraordinary late-18th-century pietà carved from walnut, and a carved and painted 1439 polyptych altarpiece by Blaž Jurjev of Trogir, considered a Croatian masterpiece. (Muzej ikona; Trg Svih Svetih; 15KN; ⊙9am-2pm Mon-Sat May-Sep)

Veliki Revelin Tower (p96)

Veliki Revelin Tower

TOWER

3 ⊙ MAP P94, C5

The main entrance to the old city is through the southern land gate at the base of this tower. Built in the 14th century and later extended, this fortification is adorned with coats of arms of the Venetian doges and Korčulan governors. There was originally a wooden drawbridge here, but it was replaced in the 18th century by the wide stone steps that give a sense of grandeur to the entrance. (Trg kralja Tomislava)

Eating

Cukarin

DELI $

4 ⊗ MAP P94, A6

This deli-style place bakes sweet Korčulan creations such as *klajun* (walnut pastry) and *amareta* (a round, rich cake with almonds). It also sells wine, jam and olive oil from the island. (🖉 020-711 055; www.cukarin.hr; Hrvatske bratske zajednice bb; cakes from 10KN; ⏱8.30am-noon & 5-7.30pm Mon-Sat Apr-Oct)

Korčula's History in Stone

Rome conquered Korčula in the 1st century, giving way to the Byzantines in the 6th and Slavs in the 7th century. After the turn of the first millennium, the island passed through the hands of various states before 1420 when it fell to the Venetians, who remained until 1797. Under Venetian control the island became known for its stone, which was quarried and cut for export. Shipbuilding also flourished.

Although documents indicate that a walled town existed on the site in the 13th century, it wasn't until the 15th that the current Korčula Town was built. Construction coincided with the apogee of stone-carving skills on the island, lending the buildings and streets a distinctive style. In the 16th century, masons added decorative flourishes such as ornate columns and coats of arms to building facades, which gave a Renaissance look to the original Gothic core.

The old town's fascinating fishbone layout was cleverly designed for the comfort and safety of its inhabitants: western streets were built straight in order to open the city to the refreshing summer *maestral* (westerly wind), while the eastern streets were curved to minimise the force of the winter *bura* (northeasterly wind).

Korčula's towers and remaining city walls look particularly striking when approached from the sea, their presence warning pirates the town would be no pushover. Originally these defences would have been even more foreboding, forming a complete stone barrier against invaders that consisted of 12 towers and 20m-high walls.

Marco Polo: Italian or Croatian?

In 2011, nearly 700 years after his death, Marco Polo was the subject of a minor diplomatic spat between Italy, Croatia and China, when former Croatian president Stjepan Mešić spoke at the opening of a museum dedicated to the explorer in Yangzhou. Mešić described Polo as a 'world explorer, born in Croatia, who opened up China to Europe'. This immediately sent the Italian media into a frenzy, accusing Croatia of the cultural theft of one of their national treasures.

While it's uncertain exactly where Marco Polo was born (both Venice and Korčula claim him), it's generally agreed that it was within the Venetian Republic. It certainly wasn't in Croatia (which was ruled by Hungary at the time and didn't include Korčula) or in Italy (which didn't exist as a state until the 19th century).

One of Korčula's historic families went by the surname Pilić (meaning 'chicken' in Croatian). It was common at the time for merchants and the aristocracy to use both Croatian and Italian versions of their names; hence Marko Pilić would become Marco Polo (*pollo* meaning 'chicken' in Italian).

Despite the lack of proof one way or another, Korčula trumpets its Marco Polo claim stridently, so much so that there are now two Marco Polo museums in town, neither of which is particularly good.

Marco's
DALMATIAN $$

5 ⊗ MAP P94, C4

The hanging tentacles of filament lights over the bar and the big brass fixtures over the tables mark this out as one of Korčula's most fresh and fun restaurants. The menu joins the party, offering traditional specialities such as *žrnovski makaruni* (hand-rolled pasta) alongside the likes of burgers and couscous salads. (☏ 098 275 701; www.marcoskorcula.com; Kaparova 1; mains 65-115KN; ⊙ 9am-midnight mid-Apr–mid-Oct, 6-11pm Mon-Sat Mar–mid-Apr & mid-Oct–Dec)

LD Terrace
DALMATIAN $$$

6 ⊗ MAP P94, D3

The LD stands for Lešić Dimitri (www.ldpalace.com) and it's no surprise that Korčula's most elegant accommodation should also have its finest restaurant. The setting is magnificent, with a chic upstairs dining room as well as romantic tables set right above the water. The modern Dalmatian menu is well matched by a fine wine list, featuring many high-quality local drops. (☏ 020-601 726; www.ldrestaurant.com; Šetalište Petra Kanavelića bb; mains 190-240KN; ⊙ 8am-midnight Apr-Oct; ☎)

Rural Eats

Our favourite place to eat on the entire island has the unlikely setting of the sleepy farming village of **Pupnat**, 11km west of Korčula Town. The menu at **Konoba Mate** (☑020-717 109; www.konobamate.hr; Pupnat 28; mains 60-118KN; ⏰11am-2pm & 7pm-midnight Mon-Sat, 7pm-midnight Sun May-Sep; 🛜) is short but universally tempting, offering unusual twists on true-blue traditions, including kid goat cooked under a *peka* (domed baking lid). The antipasto platter is sublime. And mate, the name's pronounced *ma*-teh.

It's all about the barbecue (which dad is firmly in control of) at friendly, family-run **Konoba Belin** (☑091 50 39 258; www.facebook.com/RestoranBelin; Žrnovo Prvo Selo 50; mains 50-130KN; ⏰10.30am-1.30pm & 6-11.30pm Mon-Sat, 6-11.30pm Sun May-Oct) in the old part of **Žrnovo**, 2.5km west of Korčula Town. Expect lots of grilled fish and meat; call ahead and they'll chuck octopus or lamb under the *peka*.

Everything you'd want from a rural tavern, **Konoba Maslina** (☑020-711 720; www.konobamaslina.com; Lumbarajska cesta bb; mains 65-120KN; ⏰11am-10pm Mon-Sat, to 4pm Sun; 🛜♿) offers honest country cooking including local specialties such as *žrnovski makaruni* (homemade pasta with a meaty sauce) and *pašticada* (rich beef stew). Fresh fish, lamb, veal and local cheese also feature prominently. It's about 3km out of Korčula on the road to Lumbarda.

Aterina
MEDITERRANEAN $$$

7 🍽 MAP P94, B4

As well as being a brilliant place to watch the sunset, Aterina serves an excellent selection of Italian-influenced seafood dishes. The daily specials are the main show – chalked on a blackboard to reflect the daily catch. We also love the hipsterish array of knowingly tacky plastic tablecloths. (☑091 98 61 856; www.facebook.com/aterinakorcula; Trg Korčulanskih klesara i kipara 2; mains 80-180KN; ⏰noon-midnight May-Oct)

Drinking

Vinum Bonum
WINE BAR

8 🍷 MAP P94, B6

Tucked away on a car-free lane just off the harbour, this casual place allows you to nibble on antipasti while you sample some of the island's best wine and *rakija* (grappa). (☑091 47 70 236; Punta Jurana 66; ⏰6pm-midnight May-Oct; 🛜)

Massimo

COCKTAIL BAR

MAP P94, C2

The place to be in Korčula at sunset, this adults-only bar is lodged in the turret of the Zakerjan Tower and is accessible only by ladder; the drinks are brought up by pulley. Visit for the novelty and the views, not for the tacky cocktail list. (Šetalište Petra Kanavelića 1; ⏱3-11pm May-Oct)

Entertainment

Moreška Cultural Club

DANCE

10 ⭐ MAP P94, B5

Enthusiastic townspeople perform the traditional Moreška sword dance, accompanied by a brass band, in an hour-long show. The event usually includes unaccompanied singing by a *klapa* group. (www.moreska.hr; Ljetno kino, Foša 2; 100KN; ⏱shows 9pm Mon & Thu Jul & Aug, shows 9pm Thu Jun & Sep)

Shopping

Kutak Knjiga

BOOKS

11 🔒 MAP P94, A5

It's a mystery how Kutak crams books written in Croatian, English, French, Spanish, Czech, Italian, German, Polish, Swedish and Mandarin into such a small place. It stocks a good selection of Croatian classics translated into English. (☏020-716 541; http://kutak-knjiga.blogspot.co.nz; Kovački prolaz bb; ⏱9.30am-8pm Mon-Fri May-Oct, to 1.30pm Nov-Apr)

Moreška sword dance

Explore
Hvar Town & Hvar Island

Long, lean Hvar is vaguely shaped like the profile of a holidaymaker reclining on a sun lounger, which is appropriate for the sunniest spot in the country. Historic Hvar Town has swanky hotels, multiple hostels, elegant restaurants, buzzy bars and a general sense that, if you care about seeing and being seen, this is the place to be.

You can knock off all of Hvar Town's sights in half a day, starting with a hike up to Fortica (p105) before it gets too hot. Wander down through the walled town to St Stephen's Cathedral (p105) and the Episcopal Museum (p106), then stroll along the waterfront to the Franciscan Monastery (p106). In the afternoon, either head to the Pakleni Islands for some beach time or take a trip to Stari Grad (p108), the island's oldest town. Aim to be at Hula-Hula Hvar (p111) at sunset. Grab a bite to eat, then join the party crowd at Kiva Bar (p111).

Getting There & Around

⚓ Car ferries head to Stari Grad (from Split) and to Sućuraj (from Drvenik). Catamarans head to Hvar Town (from Split and Korčula year-round, and seasonally from Bol, Mljet and Dubrovnik) and Jelsa (from Split and Bol).

🚌 Services connect Hvar Town with Stari Grad (30KN, 30 minutes) and Jelsa (33KN, 50 minutes).

Hvar Town Map on 104

Hvar Town XBRCHX/500PX ©

Top Sights 📷
Pakleni Islands

Stretched out in front of Hvar Town, the Pakleni Islands (Pakleni otoci) are a gorgeous chain of wooded isles with crystal-clear waters, hidden beaches and peaceful lagoons. Although the name is often translated as 'Hell's Islands', it's thought to derive from paklina, a pine resin that was once harvested here to waterproof boats.

Jerolim

The closest of the Pakleni Islands to Hvar, the island of **Jerolim** is entirely clothing optional. Naturism in Croatia enjoys a long and venerable history that began on Rab Island around the turn of the 20th century. It quickly became a fad among the Austrians (who ruled Croatia until 1918) influenced by the growing German *Freikörperkultur* (FKK, 'free body culture') movement. However the real trailblazers of Adriatic naturism were Edward VIII and Wallis Simpson, who popularised it by going skinny-dipping along the Rab coast in 1936.

Marinkovac

Marinkovac is best known for the raucous beach club on Stipanska bay. **Carpe Diem Beach** (☎099 49 68 534; www.carpe-diem-hvar.com; ⏱10am-7pm & 11pm-5am Jun–mid-Sep) offers quite the heady Med-glam experience, with family-friendly beach fun during the day and all-night parties after dark (boat transfers depart outside the other Carpe Diem bar in Hvar Town; admission charges vary depending on the night).

At the island's opposite end are pretty Ždrilca and lagoon-like Mlini. Both have seasonal restaurants and a handful of stone cottages.

Sveti Klement

The largest of the Pakleni Islands by far, Sveti Klement supports three villages in its 5 sq km. Palmižana is set on a beautiful horseshoe bay, with a busy marina, accommodation, restaurants and a tiny sandy beach. The artsy Meneghello family runs a beautiful boutique complex of villas and bungalows scattered among lush tropical gardens. **Palmižana Meneghello** (☎021-717 270; www.palmizana.hr; r/apt from €160/180; ❄🛜) has two restaurants and an art gallery, and often hosts music recitals.

✕ Take a Break

Palmižana has a brace of upmarket restaurants catering to the well-heeled yachties moored in the bay. **Zori** (☎091 32 22 227; www.zori.hr; Palmižana 19; mains 150-380KN; ⏱11.30am-11pm Apr-Oct) serves contemporary European cuisine, including Dalmatian specialities. The slick service and gorgeous setting, on a terrace shaded by palm trees, will help to distract you from the prices.

★ Getting There

Taxi boats leave regularly for the islands, departing from in front of the Arsenal in Hvar Town. Expect to pay around 50KN to 60KN for the nearer islands and about 70KN to 80KN for Palmižana (on Sveti Klement).

Alternatively, you can hire a boat and skipper for a two-hour cruise around the nearer islands for about 550KN.

A   B   C   D

1

Dr Josip
Avelini Park

Fortica ⊙1

Higijeničkog društva

10 ⊙   9 ⊙
Sv Marka
15 ⊙
16 ⊙   12 ⊙   19 ⊙

2

Kroz Grodu

11 ⊗ Matije Ivanića

Marije Maričić
13 ⊗
Petra Hektorovića

Dr Mate Miličića

17 ⊙

Trg Marka
Miličića

Vinka
Pribojevića

Trg Sv
Stjepana ⊙2

5 ⊙ Arsenal

Ivana Frane
Biundovića
8 ⊙

4 ⊙ Episcopal
Museum
3 ⊙ St Stephen's
Cathedral

Jurja Novaka

Vicka Butorića

Vlade Stošića

Antifašizma

Obala Fabrika

3

Hvar
Harbour

Grge Novaka ⊙7

Obala Riva

Kroz Burak

Hvarskih bratovština

Šime Buzolića Tome

Cemetery

Jelke Bučić

Šime Buzolića Tome

4

18 ⊙

14 ⊗

Šetalište put Križa

For reviews see

⊙ Sights   p105
⊗ Eating   p107
⊖ Drinking   p111

5

Ⓝ 0 ───── 200 m
   0 ───── 0.1 miles

6 ⊙ Franciscan
Monastery

6

Hvar Island

See Main Map

Hvar Town

Milna
Zaraće
Dubovica

Hvarski Channel

Bol

Stari
Grad

Vrboska

Jelsa

Sv Nikola
(626m)

Zavala

Šćedro

Adriatic Sea

Tučepi

Podgora

Igrane ⊙
Živogošće ⊙

Sućuraj

A   B   C   D

Sights

Fortica

FORTRESS

⊙ MAP P104, B1

Looming high above the town and lit with a golden glow at night, this medieval castle occupies the site of an ancient Illyrian settlement dating from before 500 BC. The views looking down over Hvar and the Pakleni Islands are magnificent, and well worth the trudge up through the old-town streets. Once you clear the town walls it's a gently sloping meander up the tree-shaded hillside to the fortress – or you can drive to the very top (100KN in a taxi). (Tvrđava Španjola; ☏021-742 608; Biskupa Jurja Dubokovica bb; adult/child 40/20KN; ⊙8am-9pm Apr-Oct)

Trg Sv Stjepana

SQUARE

2 ⊙ MAP P104, C2

Stretching from the harbour to the cathedral, this impressive rectangular square was formed by filling in an inlet that once reached out from the bay. At 4500 sq metres, it's one of the largest old squares in Dalmatia. Hvar Town's walled core, established in the 13th century, covers the slopes to the north. The town didn't spread south until the 15th century. (St Stephen's Sq)

St Stephen's Cathedral

CATHEDRAL

3 ⊙ MAP P104, C2

Providing a grand backdrop to the main square, this baroque cathedral was built in the 16th and 17th centuries at the height of the

St Stephen's Cathedral

Dalmatian Renaissance to replace a cathedral destroyed by the Turks. Parts of the older building include stone reliefs of saints near the rear of the nave and the carved 15th-century choir stalls. The most distinctive feature is its tall, rectangular bell tower, which sprouts an additional window at each level, giving it an oddly top-heavy appearance. (Katedrala svetog Stjepana; Trg Sv Stjepana bb; ⏱hours vary)

Episcopal Museum

MUSEUM

4 ◉ MAP P104, C2

Adjoining the cathedral (p105), this treasury houses silver vessels, embroidered liturgical robes, numerous Madonnas, a 13th-century icon, an elaborately carved sarcophagus and, intriguingly, a stamp collection. A highlight is a 15th-century golden chalice that was a gift from the last king of Bosnia. (Biskupski Muzej; ☎021-743 126; Trg Sv Stjepana 26; 10KN; ⏱9am-noon & 5-7pm Mon-Fri, 9am-noon Sat Jun-Sep)

Arsenal

HISTORIC BUILDIN

5 ◉ MAP P104, B3

Mentioned in Venetian document: as 'the most beautiful and the most useful building in the whole of Dalmatia', the Arsenal once served as a repair and refitting sta tion for war galleons. Its present incarnation was built in 1611 to replace a building destroyed by the Ottomans. Although you can't enter through the large, graceful arch, you can wander up the stairs to the terrace to enjoy the views over Hvar's attractive harbour. (Trg Sv Stjepana)

Franciscan Monastery

MONASTER

6 ◉ MAP P104, C5

Overlooking a pretty cove, this 15th-century monastery has an elegant bell tower, built in the 16th century by a well-known family of stonemasons from Korčula. Its Renaissance cloister leads to a refectory containing lace, coins,

Jelsa

The small harbour town of Jelsa (population 3590) is a tidy little place surrounded by thick pine forests and tall poplars. While it lacks the Renaissance buildings of Hvar Town, its intimate streets, squares and parks are pleasant, and there are some good swimming spots nearby.

Jelsa's parish church, the **Church of the Assumption** (Trg Križonoše; ⏱hours vary), has an elegant baroque facade and a Renaissance bell tower, while inside there are ceiling frescos and an elaborate marble high altar. It's been tinkered with over the centuries, but a large part of the structure dates from 1535.

Beaches around Hvar Town

Most of the swimming spots on the promenade heading west from the centre are tiny, rocky bays, some of which have been augmented with concrete sunbathing platforms. Wander along and take your pick, but check the prices before you settle on a lounger, as some are stupidly expensive (325KN per day at the historic Bonj Les Bains beach club, for instance).

If you don't mind a hike, there are larger pebbly beaches in the opposite direction. A 30-minute walk south and then east from the centre will bring you to the largest of them, **Pokonji Dol**. From here, a further 25 minutes via a scenic but rocky path will bring you to secluded **Mekićevica**.

Otherwise, grab a taxi boat to the Pakleni Islands or to one of the beaches further east along the coast such as **Milna** and **Zaraće**. **Dubovica** is particularly recommended: a tiny cluster of stone houses and a couple of cafe-bars set on a gorgeous grin of beach. The juxtaposition of the white pebbles alongside the brilliant blue-green water is dazzling. If you have your own wheels you can park on the highway, not far from where it turns inland towards the tunnel, and reach Dubovica via a rough stony path.

nautical charts and valuable documents, such as an edition of Ptolemy's *Atlas* printed in 1524. Inside, your eye will immediately be drawn to *The Last Supper,* an 8m by 2.5m work by the Venetian Matteo Ingoli that dates from the end of the 16th century. (Franjevački samostan; Šetaliste put Križa 15; museum 30KN; ⊙9am-3pm & 5-7pm Mon-Sat May-Oct)

Eating

Nonica

BAKERY $

7 ⊗ MAP P104, B3

Savour the best cakes in town at this tiny bakery. Try old-fashioned local biscuits such as *rafioli* and *forski koloc,* and the Nonica tart with chocolate mousse and orange peel. (☏021-718 041; www.nonica. com.hr; Kroz Burak 23; sweets 15-30KN; ⊙8am-2pm & 5-11pm Mon-Sat, 5-11pm Sun Apr-Oct)

Fig

CAFE $$

8 ⊗ MAP P104, C3

Run by an Aussie-Croat and an American, this great little place serves up delicious stuffed flat-breads (fig and ricotta, pear and gorgonzola, brie and prosciutto), vegetarian curries and a highly recommended Hvar breakfast: spiced eggs. There are even some vegan options – a rarity in these parts. (☏099 26 79 890;

Stari Grad

Stari Grad (population 2790), on Hvar's north coast, is a quieter, more cultured and altogether more sober affair than Hvar Town, its stylish and sybaritic sister. If you're not after pulsating nightlife and thousands of people crushing each other along the streets in the high season, head here and enjoy Hvar at a more leisurely pace. That said, you can easily see all of the little town's sights in half a day.

The name Stari Grad means 'Old Town', a reference to the fact that it was founded in 384 BC by the ancient Greeks, who called it Pharos. The surrounding fields are still divided into parcels of land demarcated in antiquity.

The town sits at the end of a deep inlet, with the narrow lanes of the old quarter spreading out on its southern side. At its centre is **St Stephen's Church** (Crkva sv Stjepana; Trg Sv Stjepana; ☾hours vary), built in the baroque style in 1605.

Nearby, **Tvrdalj** (☏021-765 068; Trg Tvrdalj Petra Hektorovića 11; 15KN; ☾10am-1pm & 5-9pm May-Oct) is a fortified house built by aristocrat and writer Petar Hektorović in the 16th century. At its heart is a lovely, lush Renaissance garden, set around the green waters of a fish pond.

Founded in 1482, the **Dominican Monastery** (Dominikanski samostan sv Petra Mučenika; ☏021-765 442; Kod Sv Petra 3; 20KN; ☾9.30am-12.30pm & 4-6.30pm May-Oct) was damaged by the Turks in 1571 and later fortified with a tower. Palms, orange trees, hydrangeas and lavender bloom in the cloister garden, and there's an interesting little museum with a painting by Tintoretto.

The waterfront promenade continues along the northern bank to a small beach and the **Eremitaž restaurant** (☏091 54 28 395; Obala hrvatskih branitelja 2; mains 60-140KN; ☾noon-3pm & 6pm-midnight May-Oct), housed in a hermitage built in 1487 for the hermit monk serving neighbouring St Jerome's Church.

---

www.figcafebar.com; Ivana Frane Biundovića 3; mains 65-100KN; ☾10am-10pm May-Oct; 🛜 ✍)

Lola

STREET FOOD $$

9 MAP P104, B2

Hit this buzzing hole-in-the-wall place for top-notch cocktails

and a globetrotting array of tasty snacks: everything from empanadas and burgers to pulled-pork steamed buns and lamb curry. Grab a table on the lane and soak up the scene. (Sv Marak 10; mains 59-119KN; ☾10am-2pm & 6pm-2am; ✍)

Mizarola

PIZZA $$

10  MAP P104, B2

Mizarola has a loyal local following, partly because it's one of the only places to open in the low season, but mainly because of its crowd-pleasing Neapolitan-style pizza. It serves other things (pasta, gnocchi, risotto, grilled meat, fish), but nothing rivals the main attraction. Head up to the roof terrace and tuck in. (☑098 799 978; www.facebook.com/mizarolahvar; Vinka Pribojevića 2; mains 55-180KN; ⊗noon-midnight; 🛜)

Konoba Menego

DALMATIAN $$

11 MAP P104, C2

This rustic old house, accessed from a steep old-town laneway, aims to be as simple and authentic as possible. The place is decked out in Hvar antiques, the service is informative, and the marinated meats, cheeses and vegetables are prepared the old-fashioned Dalmatian way. (☑021-717 411; www.menego. hr; Kroz Grodu 26; mains 105-120KN; ⊗noon-2.30pm & 6-10.30pm May-Nov)

Dalmatino

DALMATIAN $$$

12 MAP P104, B2

Calling itself a 'steak and fish house', this place is always popular – due, in part, to the handsome waiters and the free-flowing *rakija* (grappa). Thankfully, the food is also excellent; try the *gregada* (fish fillet served on potatoes with a thick, broth-like sauce). (☑091 52 93 121; www.dalmatino-hvar.com; Sv Marak 1; mains 80-265KN; ⊗11am-midnight Mon-Sat Apr-Nov; 🛜)

Stari Grad

Grande Luna

DALMATIAN $$$

13 MAP P104, C2

Grande Luna's rooftop terrace doesn't offer views per se, unless you count the blue of the Dalmatian sky offset against the stone of the surrounding buildings. It's an atmospheric setting in which to try traditional dishes, such as *hvarska gregada* (fish stew) and *crni rižoto* (squid-ink risotto). The service is excellent, too. (☎ 021-741 400; www.grandeluna.hr; Petra Hektorovića 1; mains 75-180KN; ⏱ 11am-2.30pm & 5-10.30pm; 🛜)

DiVino

MEDITERRANEAN $$$

14 MAP P104, B4

The fabulous location and one of the island's best wine lists are reason enough to splurge at this swanky restaurant. Add innovative food and dazzling views of the Pakleni Islands and you have a winning formula for a special night out. Alternatively, have some sunset snacks and wine on the gorgeous terrace. Book ahead. (☎ 091 43 77 777; www.divino.com.hr; Šetalište put Križa 1; mains 135-215KN; ⏱ noon-2pm & 6pm-midnight May-Oct)

Vrboska

A single canal and some old stone bridges have earned sweet little Vrboska (www.vrboska.info) the overblown epithet of 'the Venice of Croatia'. It's nothing like Venice – but it's well worth visiting for its enigmatic, crumbling buildings and its curvy harbour, which wiggles its tail into the aforementioned canal.

Up on the hill on the south side of town is a pair of interesting churches. Fifteenth-century **St Lawrence's** (Crkva sv Lovre; Vrboska bb; ⏱ hours vary) is crammed with valuable art, including what is believed to be a Veronese triptych above the high altar. At the top of the hill is the highly unusual **Our-Lady-of-Mercy Church-Fortress** (Crkva-tvrđava sv Marije; Vrboska bb; ⏱ hours vary). From the outside it's very much a castle, with only the cross and three bells at the top marking it out as a church. It was fortified in 1575 after the town was sacked by the Ottomans four years earlier.

Finish your trip with a wine tasting and snacks at **Vina Carić** (☎ 098 16 06 276; www.vinohvar.hr; Vrboska 211, Vrboska; ⏱ noon-7pm Mon-Sat, 4-7pm Sun May-Oct), on the banks of the canal, by the second bridge.

Vrboska is on the island's north coast, about a half-hour drive from Hvar Town.

Drinking

Kiva Bar
BAR

15 MAP P104, B2

A happening place in an alleyway just off the waterfront, Kiva is packed to the rafters most nights, with patrons spilling out and filling up the lane. DJs spin a popular mix of old-school dance, pop and hip-hop classics to an up-for-it crowd. (☏091 51 22 343; www.facebook.com/kivabar.hvar; Obala Fabrika 10; ⏰9pm-2am Apr-Dec)

Nautica
BAR

16 MAP P104, B2

It starts slowly, with a mixed crowd enjoying cocktails by the water, but once Hula-Hula winds down and Kiva packs out, Nautica comes into its own as an obligatory stop on Hvar's night-crawl circuit. DJs spin everything from techno to hip hop to Euro-disco. (www.nautica-bar.com; Obala Fabrika 8; ⏰5pm-2am)

3 Pršuta
WINE BAR

17 MAP P104, C2

Hvar's best wine bar is an unpretentious little place lurking in an alley behind the main square. Sink into the couch by the bar and feel as if you're in a local's living room while sampling some of the best island wines, paired with Dalmatian snacks. (Petra Hektorovića 5; ⏰6pm-2am May-Oct)

Hula-Hula Hvar

The spot to catch the sunset to the sound of techno and house music, **Hula-Hula** (☏095 91 11 871; www.hulahulahvar.com; Šetalište Antuna Tomislava Petrića 10; ⏰9am-11pm Apr-Oct) is known for its après-beach party (4pm to 9pm), where all of Hvar's party crowd seems to descend for sundowner cocktails. Dancing on tables is pretty much compulsory.

Carpe Diem
COCKTAIL BAR

18 MAP P104, B4

Look no further – you have arrived at the mother of Croatia's glitzy coastal bars. From breakfast to (pricey) late-night cocktails, there's no time of day when this swanky place is dull. The house music spun by resident DJs is smooth, the drinks well mixed, and the crowd well heeled. (☏021-742 369; www.carpe-diem-hvar.com; Obala Riva bb; ⏰9am-2am mid-May–Sep)

Central Park Club
BAR

19 MAP P104, B2

Set behind the cluster of phoenix palms on the waterfront, this large terrace bar is Hvar's main locale for live music. In summer there's something on every night, from jazz to soul, old-time rock'n'oll and funk. Good cocktails. (☏021-718 337; www.klubparkhvar.com; Bankete bb; ⏰7am-2am Apr-Oct, to 11pm Nov-Mar)

Bol & Brač Island

Brač is the largest island in central Dalmatia, with several towns and villages, and a dramatic landscape of steep cliffs, inky waters and pine forests. The two main centres, Supetar and Bol, are quite different: Supetar is pleasant if unassuming, while Bol revels in its more exclusive appeal.

Start with an early-morning swim at Zlatni Rat (p114) before hitting the road and heading to the Blaca Hermitage (p119) and Vidova Gora lookout (p115). Continue on to Supetar for lunch and a quick look around before circling back to Bol via the Island of Brač Museum (p120) at Škrip and Pučišća. That evening, see if you can squeeze in a pre-dinner wine tasting at Stina (p117) or a blast around the Branislav Dešković Art Gallery (p117).

Getting There & Around

⚓ Car ferries head to Supetar from Split, and to Sumartin from Makarska. High-speed catamarans head to Bol year-round from Split and seasonally from Makarska, Hvar, Korčula, Mljet and Dubrovnik

🚌 Supetar is the hub, with services to Bol (43KN, one hour) and other towns.

✈ Brač airport, 14km northeast of Bol, only has scheduled flights from mid-May to September.

Bol Map on p116

Bol DREAMER4787/SHUTTERSTOCK ©

Top Sights 📷
Zlatni Rat

Croatia's most photographed beach extends like a tongue into the sea for about 400m. Despite the hype and constant crowds, the 'golden cape' is a gorgeous place. Made up of white pebbles, its elegant tip is constantly shuffled by the wind and waves. Pine trees provide shade and rocky cliffs rise behind it, giving it one of Dalmatia's loveliest settings.

 MAP P116, A3

Put Zlatnog rata

This shady 1.5km pedestrian promenade links Zlatni Rat to the historic centre of the pretty town of Bol, following the waterline all the way. The route is lined with pine trees and interesting sculpture, and in summer stalls sprout up, selling trinkets and ice creams, and touting tours and activities. As you near the beach you'll pass a trio of large hotels run by the Bluesun group.

Windsurfing

Bol is a windsurfing hot spot, with much of the action centred on Zlatni Rat. Although the *maestral* (strong, steady westerly wind) blows from April to October, the best times to windsurf are the end of May and the beginning of June, and the end of July and the beginning of August. The wind generally reaches its peak in the early afternoon and then dies down at the end of the day.

Big Blue Sport (021-635 614; www.bigblue sport.com; Plaža Borak bb; 9am-7pm Apr-Oct), based on a beach 700m east of Zlatni Rat, rents windsurfing gear (per hour/half-day €18/40) and offers six-hour beginners' courses (€135). It also rents stand-up paddleboards, kayaks and mountain bikes.

Vidova Gora

For a completely different perspective on the beach, head up to the island's highest point, **Vidova Gora** (Map p116; 778m). From here the entire island of Hvar is spread out like a map, with Zlatni Rat in the foreground and Vis and the mountains of the Pelješac Peninsula and Biokovo filling the horizon. It's easily reached by a good sealed road through a pine forest (look for the turnoff southeast of Nerežišća) or sweat your way up from Bol on foot (two hours) or by mountain bike.

★ **Top Tips**

o If you want to avoid the worst of the *maestral* (westerly wind), you're best to hit the beach in the morning or late in the afternoon.

o A small section of beach immediately west of the cape is set aside for nudists. It doesn't offer much privacy, though.

✕ **Take a Break**

The best option for a meal is **Konoba Mali Raj** (098 756 922; www.maliraj-bol. com; Zlatnog rata 56; mains 75-200KN; noon-11pm May-Sep), located just above the beach, by the car park. This alfresco tavern has a shady garden and serves delicious Dalmatian dishes such as grilled squid and fish.

There are various places where you can order drinks on the beach itself, the most stylish of which is the **Auro** cocktail bar.

Bol & Brač Island

Put Sv Lucije

Tina Ujevi

Anđelka Rabadana

Dominican Monastery **4** ⊙

David Cesta

Hrvatskih Domobrana

Our-Lady-of-Carmel Church

Branislav Dešković Art Gallery

Ante Starčevića

Novi Put

2 ⊙

3 ⊙

Riva Frane Radića

Uz Pjacu

8

6 ⊗

7 ⊗ **1** ⊙ Stina

Obala Vladimira Nazora

Ivana Mažuranića

5 ⊗

Bračka Cesta

Bračka Domovinskog Rata

Put Zlatnog Rata

Put Oleandera

Zlatni Rat ⊙

For reviews see

⊙ Top Sights	p114
⊙ Sights	p117
⊗ Eating	p119
⊕ Drinking	p121

0   500 m
0   0.25 miles

Island of Brač map

Split

Sutivan

Supetar

Splitska

Škrip

Island of Brač Museum

Postira

Dol

Mimice

Pisak

Bračand Channel

Pučišća

Pražnica

Gornji Humac

Selca

Sumartin

Makarska

Donji Humac

Nerežišća

Ložišća

Milna

Blaca Hermitage

Dragon's Cave

Vidova Gora

Brač Airport ✈

BOL

Jelsa

Hvar, Korčula; Dubrovnik

Hvar; Vis

See Main Map

Hvarski Channel

Brac

Split

0   5 miles
0   10 km

Sights

Stina

WINERY

1 ◎ MAP P116, D2

This local winery operates a slick, modern tasting room in the First Dalmatian Wine Co-op warehouse (built in 1903), right on the waterfront. Call in at 5pm for a 30-minute tour and leisurely tasting of its top drops, including indigenous Croatian varietals *pošip*, *vugava*, *tribidrag* and *plavac mali*. Otherwise, just drop by for a glass of wine in elegant surrounds. (☏021-306 220; www.stina-vino.hr; Riva bb; tastings 75-295KN; ◷11am-7pm Apr, to 9pm May & Oct, to midnight Jun-Sep)

Branislav Dešković Art Gallery

GALLERY

2 ◎ MAP P116, E1

Housed in a Renaissance-baroque town house right on the seafront, this excellent gallery displays paintings and sculptures by 20th-century Croatian artists. It's a surprisingly prestigious collection for such a small town, including works by such luminaries as sculptor Ivan Meštrović and expressionist painter Ignjat Job. The gallery is named after Brač-born Dešković (1883–1939), a sculptor who became famous for his depictions of animals – look for his *Scratching Dog* in the courtyard. (Galerija umjetnina Branislav Dešković; ☏021-637 092; Trg Sv Petra 1; adult/child 15/5KN;

Bol & Brač Island Sights

Blaca Hermitage (p119)

Supetar

Although it suffers in comparison to its more glitzy sister, Bol, Supetar (population 4080) is an attractive town in its own right, with a historic core of old stone streets fanning out from a harbour dominated by the imposing 18th-century **Church of the Annunciation** (Crkva Navještenja Marijina; Radnička 4; ☺hours vary). It's a popular holiday destination for Croatian families, with various pebbly beaches within an easy stroll of the town centre.

An unexpected highlight of Supetar is its fascinating **cemetery** (Groblje Supetar; Banj bb), full of striking sculptural monuments. Grandest of all is the over-the-top Petrinović family mausoleum. Built from white Brač stone between 1924 and 1927, it has a cluster of five Byzantine-style domes, an ornate bronze door and a fine carved relief in the style of the Vienna Succession. Just outside the main entrance are the ruins of a 6th-century Roman house.

Head to **Beer Garden** (☏095 55 67 225; www.facebook.com/beergardensupetar; Petra Jakšića 1; ☺8am-midnight May-Oct), tucked away in the old town, to listen to indie tunes, sample from a big selection of local and imported craft beer, and snack on food such as boar and venison burgers. Another great option is **Vinotoka** (☏021-630 969; Jobova 6; mains 70-150KN; ☺noon-10pm Apr-Sep; ☎), where you can feast on seafood by the open fire in the stone-walled dining room or, when it warms up, grab a table on the street.

☺9am-noon & 6-11pm Tue-Sun Jul & Aug, 9am-3pm Tue-Sat Sep-Jun)

Our-Lady-of-Carmel Church
CHURCH

3 ◉ MAP P116, E1

Bol's main parish church is a pretty baroque structure built between 1668 and 1788. The sturdy stone exterior is ornamented with a frilly pediment set with a clock, a finely sculpted rose window and a stone angel holding Veronica's veil over the door. Inside there are ornate baroque altars and a delicate marble pulpit. (Župna crkva Gospe od Karmela; Uz pjacu bb; ☺hours vary)

Dominican Monastery
MONASTERY

4 ◉ MAP P116, F2

Positioned at the end of a pretty pebbly beach, this monastery was founded in 1475, but it's far from the oldest structure on the site; the little chapel by the beach was built in the 9th or 10th century on 6th-century foundations. Although it's often closed, the main church has a magnificent altar painting from the workshop of Venetian superstar Tintoretto. There's also a museum displaying rare manuscripts, coins, liturgical items and archaeological finds. (Dominikanski samostan; Šetalište Anđelka Rabadana 4; ⏰hours vary)

preorder spit-roasted lamb or a *peka* (traditional roasting dome) filled with lamb, veal or octopus. And make sure you say hi to the loud-mouthed parrot. (📞021-635 635; Hrvatskih domobrana 6; mains 55-190KN; ⏰6-11.30pm)

Eating

Ranč DALMATIAN $$

5 🍴 MAP P116, C1

The simple things stand out at Ranč, such as the delicious homemade bread and the traditional fish soup. Call ahead to

Taverna Riva DALMATIAN $$$

6 🍴 MAP P116, D1

Bol's most upmarket and expensive restaurant serves fancy Frenchified versions of Dalmatian dishes, including a delicious fish soup, creamy seafood pastas, gnocchi with truffles, lobster and

Blaca Hermitage

Things can't have looked too different on the approach to this remote mountain **hermitage** (Pustinje Blaca; Map p116, C4; 📞091 51 64 671; adult/child 40/10KN; ⏰9am-5pm Tue-Sun Jul & Aug, to 3pm Tue-Sun Sep-Jun) when a small group of priests and their servants, on the run from the Ottoman Turks, arrived here in 1551. They initially took shelter in a cave (the walls of which are still visible in the kitchen) and built out from there. You can now take an informative 30-minute tour of the complex, which is full of original furniture, tools and rare manuscripts.

By the 18th century the hermitage ministered to three remote villages, with the priests operating a school from one of the rooms. The school closed in 1963 with the death of the hermitage's last resident priest, the extraordinary Fr Nikola Miličević, who was also a poet and an astronomer of international repute.

The journey is a large part of the experience, involving a rough drive along a narrow, unsealed road and then a 2.5km walk down a steep path (good shoes are recommended). The turnoff is well signposted from the main island road southeast of Nerežišća; it's the same turnoff as for the Vidova Gora lookout, and the two can easily be combined into one trip. Alternatively, you can arrange a boat from Bol to the bottom of the valley and walk up.

Brač's Quiet Escapes

Sumartin, the entry point to Brač if you're coming from Makarska, is a sleepy port with a few rocky beaches and little to do, but it makes a nice retreat from the busier tourist centres.

For a quiet coastal getaway, head to **Pučišća** (try saying that quickly three times after a shot of *rakija!*) on Brač's northern coast. This appealing little town curves around a port lined with blindingly white historic buildings. One of these, the 15th-century **Palača Desković** (021-778 240; www.palaca-deskovic.com; Trg Sv Jeronima 4; s/d from €154/206; P ❄ 🤍), has been converted into a particularly atmospheric hotel. Another, nearby, houses the **tourist office** (021-633 555; www.tzo-pucisca.hr; Trg Hrvatskog skupa 1; 8am-noon Mon-Fri May & Oct, to 2pm Mon-Sat Jun & Sep, to 8pm daily Jul & Aug).

One of Brač's more interesting sites is the village of **Škrip**, the oldest settlement on the island, about 8km southeast of Supetar. Formerly a refuge of the ancient Illyrians, the fort was taken over by the Romans in the 2nd century BC, and then by refugees escaping the fall of Salona (near Split). The **Island of Brač Museum** (Brački otoka muzej; Map p116, D3; 091 63 70 920; adult/child 20/10KN; 9am-7pm) is housed in the Kaštil Radojković, a tower built during the Venetian-Turkish wars that incorporates part of an ancient Illyrian wall and a surprisingly intact Roman mausoleum.

Donji Humac, 8km south of Supetar, has a stone quarry and an interesting onion-domed church tower. However, the main reason to head here is to enjoy the panoramic valley views at **Konoba Kopačina** (021-647 707; www.konoba-kopacina.com; Donji Humac 7; mains 40-140KN; 10am-10pm Mon-Thu, to midnight Fri & Sat; 🤍 🗡) while sampling traditional Brač specialities such as *vitalac* (skewered lamb offal wrapped in lamb meat).

The port of **Milna**, 20km southwest of Supetar, is the kind of lovely intact fishing village that in any other part of the world would have long ago been commandeered by package tourists. For now, though, it's mainly visited by luxury yachts. The 17th-century town is set at the edge of a deep natural harbour that was used by Emperor Diocletian for shipping stone to Split for the construction of his palace. Paths head around the harbour, which is studded with coves containing rocky beaches. Dominating the picture-perfect setting is the tall steeple of the beautiful 18th-century **Church of the Annunciation** (Riva bb; hours vary), with a baroque facade, pretty painted ceiling and ornate marble altars.

Dragon's Cave

It takes about an hour to hike to this strange **cave** (Zmajeva špilja; Map p116, D4; 📞091 51 49 787; per person 50KN, minimum 200KN) from Murvica, 5km west of Bol, where an extremely unusual set of reliefs decorates the walls. Believed to have been sculpted by an imaginative 15th-century friar, the carvings include angels, animals and a gaping dragon. The cave can only be accessed on a guided tour; either call Zoran Kojdić directly or ask at the tourist office. You'll need decent walking shoes.

a selection of steaks. Try to leave room for the walnut semifreddo. It's located on a pretty terrace right above the *riva* (seafront promenade). (📞021-635 236; www.tavernariva-bol.com; Frane Radića 5; mains 95-370KN; ⊙noon-3pm & 6-10pm Mar-Oct; 🖉)

during the day and return in the evening for fab cocktails, DJs and lounging on sofas and armchairs. (📞091 23 33 471; www.facebook.com/Varadero.Bol; Frane Radića 1; ⊙8am-2am May-Nov; 🛜)

Drinking

Marinero　　　　　　BAR

7 🚉 MAP P116, D1

A popular gathering spot for Bol locals, with a leafy terrace on a square, an upmarket interior, football on the TV, Bon Jovi on the stereo, regular live music and a diverse merry-making crowd. (📞021-635 579; www.facebook.com/marinerobol; Rudina 46; ⊙8am-2am; 🛜)

Varadero　　　　COCKTAIL BAR

8 🚉 MAP P116, E1

At this open-air cocktail bar on the seafront you can sip coffee and fresh OJ under straw umbrellas

Portside restaurants, Bol

PAWEL KAZMIERCZAK/SHUTTERSTOCK ©

Explore ⊛
Split

Croatia's second-largest city, Split (Spalato in Italian, population 178,000) is a great place to see Dalmatian life as it's really lived. Always buzzing, this exuberant city has just the right balance between history and modernity. Daily life and commerce hums along within the ancient walls of Diocletian's Palace as it has done for millennia.

Start by thoroughly exploring Diocletian's Palace (p124). Take a look around the Split City Museum (p136) and, time allowing, the Gallery of Fine Arts (p136) before heading to the Veli Varoš neighbourhood for lunch at one of its excellent seafood restaurants. Take a stroll up to Marjan Forest Park (p133) for the views. From here you can either press on to Kašjuni beach (p133) for a swim, or wander back down to the city and head to the Archaeological Museum (p138). Finish up with a meal and drink in the old town.

Getting There & Around

✈ Dozens of airlines fly here from all over Europe.

🚌 Intercity and international buses arrive at the main bus station beside the harbour.

⚓ Split is a major ferry port, with services to Italy, the Dalmatian islands, Trogir, Makarska and Dubrovnik.

🚆 Four trains a day travel between Split and Zagreb (194KN, 6½ hours).

Split Map on p134

Trg Republike, Split DREAMER4787/SHUTTERSTOCK ©

Top Sights 📷
Diocletian's Palace

Taking up a prime harbourside position, this extraordinary complex is one of the most imposing ancient Roman structures in existence today, and where you'll spend most of your time while in Split. Don't expect a palace, though, nor a museum – this is the city's living heart, its labyrinthine streets packed with people, bars, shops and restaurants.

◎ MAP P134, G4

Walls & Gates

Built as a combined imperial residence, military fortress and fortified town, the palace measures 215m from north to south and 180m east to west, altogether covering 38,700 sq metres. Although the original structure has been added to continuously over the millennia, the alterations have only served to increase the allure of this fascinating site.

Diocletian – the first Roman emperor to abdicate voluntarily – commissioned this magnificent palace to be completed in time for his retirement in AD 305. It was built from lustrous white stone transported from the island of Brač, and construction lasted 10 years. Diocletian spared no expense, importing marble from Italy and Greece, and columns and 12 sphinxes from Egypt.

Each wall has a gate at its centre that's named after a metal: the elaborate northern **Golden Gate** (Zlatna Vrata; Dioklecijanova bb), the southern **Bronze Gate** (Brončana Vrata; Obala hrvatskog narodnog preporoda bb), the eastern **Silver Gate** (Srebrna Vrata) and the western **Iron Gate** (Željezna Vrata). Between the eastern and western gates there's a straight road (Krešimirova, also known as Decumanus), which separated the imperial residence on the southern side, with its state rooms and temples, from the northern side, once used by soldiers and servants.

Bronze Gate & Substructure

Although it's easy to lose sight of the palace amid the bustle of Split's waterfront promenade, take time to step back and look up. The original arches and columns of the palace wall can be easily discerned above the shops and restaurants. It would have presented a magnificent face to the sea, with the water lapping at the base of the walls. It's not hard to see why Diocletian built his imperial apartments on this

★ Top Tips

○ A ticket for the cathedral (p127) includes admission to its crypt, treasury and baptistery (ie the Temple of Jupiter), but you'll need to pay separately to climb the bell tower.

○ In summer, visitor access to the cathedral is via the sacristy, situated in an annexe around the right-hand side of the building. In the low season, entry is via the front door and the treasury isn't open to the public (tickets are 10KN cheaper when the treasury is closed).

✕ Take a Break

Tucked into the ground floor of a 15th-century Gothic house in the northern part of the palace, Marcvs Marvlvs Spalatensis (p140) is a great place for wine and a snack.

The best place to eat within the palace precinct is upmarket Zoi (p139), a modern Mediterranean restaurant clinging to the walls.

south-facing side of the palace, gazing directly out over the water.

The unassuming Bronze Gate once opened straight from the water into the palace basements, enabling goods to be unloaded directly from ships and stored here. Now this former tradesman's entrance is the main way into the palace from the Riva.

While the central part of the **substructure** (Supstrukcije Dioklecijanove palače; www.mgst.net; Obala hrvatskog narodnog preporoda bb; adult/child 42/22KN; ☉8.30am-9pm Apr-Sep, to 5pm Sun Oct, 9am-5pm Mon-Sat, to 2pm Sun Nov-Apr) is now a major thoroughfare lined with souvenir stalls, entry to the chambers on either side is ticketed. Although mostly empty save the odd sarcophagus or bit of column, the basement rooms and corridors exude a haunting timelessness that's worth the price of admission. For fans of *Game of Thrones*, here be dragons – Daenerys Targaryen keeps her scaly brood here when she's in Meereen.

Peristil & Vestibule

From the substructure, stairs lead up to the ceremonial heart of the palace, a picturesque colonnaded ancient Roman courtyard (or peristyle; **peristil** in Croatian). In summer you can almost be guaranteed a pair of strapping local lads dressed as legionaries adding to the scene. Sitting between the columns near the cathedral is a black-granite Egyptian sphinx, dating from the 15th century BC.

At the southern end of the peristyle, above the basement stairs,

Peristil

Life Within the Palace Walls

Nowadays there are 220 buildings within the palace boundaries, home to about 3000 people. The narrow streets hide passageways and courtyards – some deserted and eerie, others thumping with music from bars and cafes – while residents hang out their washing overhead, kids kick footballs against the ancient walls, and grannies sit in their windows watching the action below.

Jews have lived in Split since ancient times, as the discovery of carvings of menorahs on the walls of the palace cellars attests. However, it was during Venetian rule that Sephardic Jews, refugees from Spain, settled here. As in Venice, they were allotted their own quarter: in this case, in the palace's northwestern corner, in houses that were left empty following an outbreak of plague.

Split's **synagogue** (☏ 021-345 672; www.zost.hr; Židovski prolaz 1; ☉ by arrangement) is the third-oldest in Europe that's still in active use. It was created out of the upper floors of two medieval houses in the 16th century, but its current appearance dates from around 1728. Today's Jewish community numbers around 100 members, but there's no permanent rabbi.

is the **vestibule** – a grand and cavernous domed room, open to the sky, which was once the formal entrance to the imperial apartments. If you're lucky, you might come across a *klapa* singing group here, taking advantage of the acoustics for an a cappella performance. Beyond the vestibule and curving around behind the cathedral are the ruins of various Roman structures, including the **triclinium** (dining hall), a bathhouse and, built into the Split Ethnographic Museum (p137), the emperor's bedroom.

Cathedral of St Domnius

Dominating one side of the peristyle, Split's octagonal **cathedral** (Katedrala sv Duje; Peristil bb; cathedral/belfry 35/20KN; ☉8am-8pm

Jun-Sep, 7am-noon & 5-7pm May & Oct, 7am-noon Nov-Feb, 8am-5pm Mar & Apr) is one of the best-preserved ancient Roman buildings still standing today. It was built as a mausoleum for Diocletian, who was interred here in AD 311. As emperor he was the last famous persecutor of the Christians, but his victims got the last laugh. In the 5th century Diocletian's sarcophagus was destroyed and his tomb converted into a church dedicated to an early bishop, martyred in Salona's amphitheatre in AD 304.

The exterior of the building is still encircled by an original colonnade of 24 columns. A much later addition, the tall Romanesque **bell tower**, was constructed between the 13th and 16th centuries and reconstructed in 1908 after it collapsed. Tickets are sold separately for those eager to climb up for views over the old town's rooftops. You'll need a head for heights, though, as the steep stone stairs quickly give way to flimsy metal ones suspended over the internal void.

Inside the cathedral, the domed interior has two rows of Corinthian columns and a frieze running high up on the walls that, surprisingly, still includes images of the emperor and his wife. To the left of the main altar is the **altar of St Anastasius** (Sveti Staš; 1448), carved by Juraj Dalmatinac. It features a relief of *The Flagellation of Christ* that is considered one of the finest sculptural works of its time in Dalmatia.

The **choir** is furnished with 13th-century Romanesque seats, the oldest of their kind in Dalmatia.

Other highlights include a 13th-century **pulpit**; the **right-hand altar**, carved by Bonino da Milano in 1427; and the **vault** above the high altar, decorated with murals by Dujam Vušković. As you leave, take a look at the remarkable scenes from the life of Christ on the wooden **entrance doors**. Carved by Andrija Buvina in the 13th century, the images are presented in 28 squares, 14 on each side, and recall the fashion of Romanesque miniatures of the time.

The cathedral's **treasury**, open only in the high season, is located in the attached sacristy and is rich in reliquaries, icons, church robes, illuminated manuscripts and documents in Glagolitic script.

Don't forget to take a look in the **crypt**, accessed by an exterior door on the right side of the church. Now

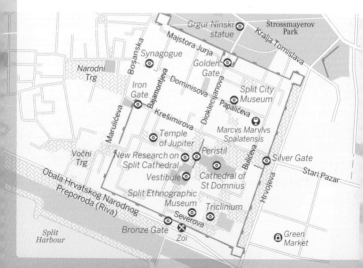

From Palace to City

Split achieved fame when the Roman emperor Diocletian (AD 245–313), noted for his restructure of the empire and persecution of early Christians, had his retirement palace built here between 295 and 305. After his death the great stone palace continued to be used as a retreat by Roman rulers. When the nearby colony of Salona (now Solin) was abandoned in the 7th century, many of the Romanised inhabitants fled to Split and barricaded themselves behind the high palace walls, where their descendants live to this day.

First the Byzantine Empire and then Croatia controlled the area, but from the 12th to the 14th centuries medieval Split enjoyed a large measure of autonomy, which favoured its development. The western part of the old town around Narodni trg, which dates from this time, became the focus of municipal life, while the area within the palace walls remained the ecclesiastical centre.

In 1420 the Venetian conquest of Split led to its slow decline. During the 17th century, strong walls were built around the city as a defence against the Ottomans. In 1797 the Austrians arrived, remaining until 1918.

a chapel dedicated to St Lucy, it's an eerily quiet chamber that stays cool even on the hottest days.

If you're interested in the technical aspects of the building's architecture, check out the free exhibition **New Research on Split Cathedral** (Nova istraživanja Splitske katedrale; Peristil bb; admission free; 10am-1pm & 5-8pm Tue-Sun) in the building opposite the main entrance.

Temple of Jupiter

Although it's now the cathedral's baptistery, this wonderfully intact building was originally an ancient Roman **temple** (Jupiterov hram; 10KN, with cathedral ticket free; 8am-7pm Mon-Sat, 12.30-6.30pm Sun May-Oct, to 5pm Nov-Apr) dedicated to the king of the gods. It still has its original barrel-vaulted ceiling and decorative frieze, although a striking bronze statue of St John the Baptist by Ivan Meštrović now fills the spot where Jupiter once stood. The font is made from 13th-century carved stones recycled from the cathedral's rood screen.

Of the columns that once supported a porch, only one remains. The black-granite sphinx guarding the entrance was defaced (literally) by early Christians, who considered it a pagan icon.

Walking Tour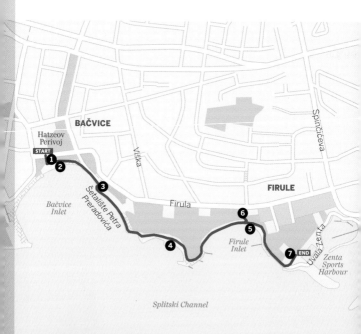

Bačvice & Firule Beach Life

In the summertime, the Splitčani leave their
ancient city centre to the tourists and head to the
beaches abutting their home suburbs, where they
socialise and cool off. A younger crowd returns in
the evening for the bars and clubs. The first batch
of beaches to the east of the harbour are the most
popular.

Walk Facts
Start Žbirac
Finish Zenta
Length 1.2km, one hour

❶ Coffee at Žbirac

Perched above Bačvice beach, **Žbirac** (Šetalište Petra Preradovića 1b; ⏰7am-midnight; 📶) is like an open-air living room – a no-nonsense place in which to chug coffee, chain-smoke and catch up on all the gossip.

❷ Bačvice Beach

Sandy **Bačvice** is Split's busiest beach, lined with restaurants, bars, late-night clubs and a whole heap of concrete. Keep an eye out for people thrashing about in the shallows, whacking a squash ball to each other with the palms of their hands: this is the very Dalmatian sport of *picigin,* a prime showing-off opportunity for Split's young bucks.

❸ Zora Bila

After spending years building a reputation as a neighbourhood tavern in a non-touristy part of town, **Zora Bila** (📞021-782 711; Šetalište Petra Preradovića 2; mains 65-110KN; ⏰1-5pm & 8-11pm Tue-Sun) moved to a prime spot above Bačvice beach. Call in to sample from its ever-changing menu of homemade pasta and grilled meats.

❹ Ovčice Beach

The next bay along the promenade, **Ovčice** (Šetalište Petra Preradovića bb) has a little less concrete, a beach bar and a pleasant strip of fine pebbles.

❺ Firule Beach

The horseshoe cove of **Firule** has a slimline sandy beach with a bar down the far end. There's not much space to spread out, but the cliffs and pine trees make for a much more appealing backdrop than Bačvice's concrete jungle.

❻ Dinner at Dvor

When you're done with the beach, head up the stairs to **Dvor** (📞021-571 513; www.facebook.com/Dvor.Split; Firula 14; breakfast 30-35KN; lunch 70-90KN, 5-course dinner 170KN; ⏰8am-midnight), an upmarket cafe and restaurant set in an elegant old house and its leafy gardens. It's a great spot for a post-beach coffee or wine – or freshen up and return later in the evening to indulge in its sophisticated, contemporary, five-course menu.

❼ Clubbing at Zenta

Dance the rest of your night away at **Zenta** (📞099 33 51 979; www.zentasplit.com; Uvala Zenta 3; 20-80KN; ⏰from 11pm, nights vary), a two-storey nightclub with a waterfront terrace overlooking the harbour of the same name. Big-name DJs occasionally hit the decks in summer, filling in the gaps between regular party nights such as Monday Trash and Friday's Recesija (cheap drinks, R&B, electronica and Balkan pop).

Walking Tour 🥾

Marjan Hill Hike

Punctuating the end of the Split peninsula, 178m-high Marjan Hill occupies a big space in the city's psyche, providing both a scenic backdrop and a place to escape the crowds. Meje, on its southern slopes, is Split's most desirable suburb. Sandwiched between the hill's eastern slopes and the old town are the tight medieval lanes of Veli Varoš.

Walk Facts

Start Zapadna Obala
Finish Veli Varoš
Length 8km, four hours

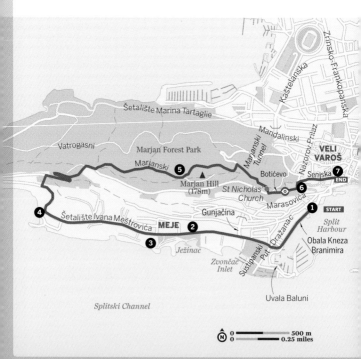

1 Zapadna Obala

As you stroll along sunny **Zapadna Obala**, the 'west coast' promenade, stop to read the tributes to Croatia's Olympians set into the pavement.

2 Meštrović Gallery

Passing through the seaside suburb of Meje, you can see why Croatia's premier modern sculptor, Ivan Meštrović, chose to build a mansion here. Now a stellar **gallery** (Galerija Meštrović; ☎021-340 800; www.mestrovic.hr; Šetalište Ivana Meštrovića 46; adult/child 40/20KN; ⏰9am-7pm Tue-Sun May-Sep, to 4pm Tue-Sun Oct-Apr) showcasing an important collection of his work, the 1930s house and gardens are open to visitors; wander through and imagine the pre-war life of Split's rich and famous.

3 Meštrović Kaštilac

The gallery ticket includes admission to this 16th-century fortified house, or **Kaštilac** (☎021-340 800; www.mestrovic.hr; Šetalište Ivana Meštrovića 39; adult/child 40/20KN, with Meštrović Gallery free; ⏰9am-7pm Tue-Sun May-Sep), set in an olive grove further up the road. It was bought by Meštrović in 1939 and restored to house his powerful *Life of Christ* cycle of wood reliefs in the chapel. Linger in the lovely quadrangle alongside the large stone sculpture.

4 Kašjuni Beach

Cool off at **Kašjuni** (Šetalište Ivana Meštrovića bb), near the tip of the peninsula. It's Split's most appealing beach, due to its green surroundings and upmarket beach bar.

5 Marjan Forest Park

Covering the bulk of Marjan Hill, this protected **forest park** (Park-šuma Marjan; www.marjan-parksuma. hr) is criss-crossed with fragrant pine-shaded paths and dotted with medieval votive chapels. The views over the islands from the giant cross and Croatian flag at the summit are extraordinary. At the Kašjuni end, look out for the cave dwellings once inhabited by Christian hermits. You might also spot climbers nearby.

6 Vidilica

Grab a seat on the terrace of this popular **cafe-bar** (Nazorov Prilaz 1; ⏰8am-midnight; 📶), situated at the eastern entrance to the park, for phenomenal views over the old town and sprawling city. Directly behind it is a venerable Jewish cemetery, founded in 1573, with gravestones poking up picturesquely between the trees.

7 Veli Varoš

Take the stairs down through the historic Veli Varoš quarter, Split's oldest suburb. Traditionally populated by fisherfolk, it still has some of the city's best seafood *konobe* (taverns).

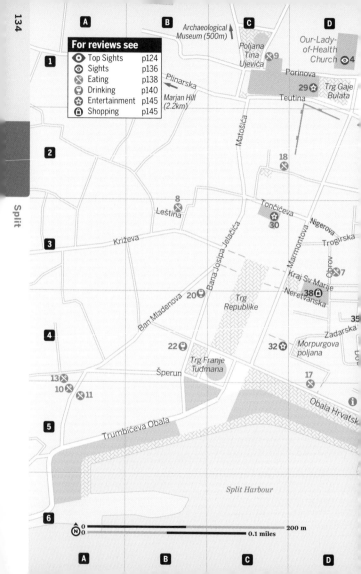

Split

For reviews see

Archaeological
Museum (500m)

Plinarska

Marjan Hill
(2.2km)

Poljana
Tina
Ujevića ✷9

Our-Lady-
of-Health
Church ◉4

Porinova

29 ✷

Trg Gaje
Bulata

Teutina

Matošića

18 ✷

Tončićeva

8 ✷
Leština

30 ✷

Nigerova

Trogirska

Obrov

7 ✷

Kraj Sv Marije

38 🛍

Neretvanska

Marmontova

Križeva

Bana Josipa Jelačića

20 🥤

Trg
Republike

Ban Mladenova

22 🥤

Trg Franje
Tuđmana

Šperun

32 ✷

Morpurgova
poljana

Zadarska

35

17 ✷

13 ✷
10 ✷ ✷11

Obala Hrvatsk

ℹ

Trumbićeva Obala

Split Harbour

▲N 0   200 m
    0   0.1 miles

A   B   C   D

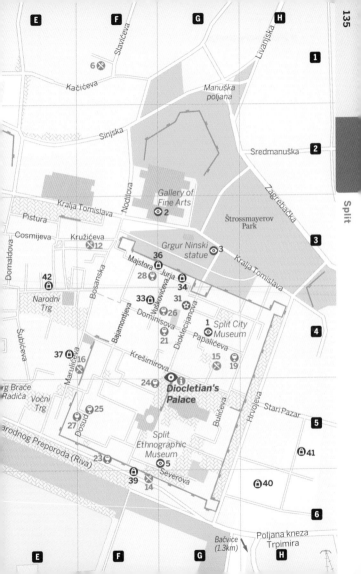

Sights

Split City Museum
MUSEUM

1 MAP P134, G4

Built by Juraj Dalmatinac in the 15th century for one of the many noblemen who lived within the old town, the Large Papalić Palace is considered a fine example of late-Gothic style, with an elaborately carved entrance gate that proclaimed the importance of its original inhabitants. The interior has been thoroughly restored to house this museum, which has interesting displays on Diocletian's Palace (p124) and on the development of the city. (Muzej grada Splita; 021-360 171; www.mgst.net; Papalićeva 1; adult/child 22/12KN; 8.30am-9pm Apr-Sep, 9am-5pm Tue-Sat, to 2pm Sun Oct-Mar)

The Riva

The ever-frenetic waterfront promenade – officially called Obala hrvatskog narodnog preporoda (Croatian National Revival Waterfront) but more commonly known as the Riva – is your best central reference point in Split. East of here, past the wharf, are the buzzy beaches of Bačvice, Firule, Zenta and Trstenik bays. The wooded Marjan Hill dominates the view to the west.

Gallery of Fine Arts
GALLERY

2 MAP P134, G3

Housed in a building that was the city's first hospital (1792), this gallery exhibits 400 works of art spanning 700 years. Upstairs is the permanent collection – a chronological journey that starts with religious icons and continues with works by the likes of Paolo Veneziano, Albrecht Dürer and Guido Reni, alongside the work of locals such as Vlaho Bukovac, Ivan Meštrović and Cata Dujšin-Ribar. The temporary exhibits downstairs change every few months. (Galerija umjetnina Split; 021-350 110; www.galum.hr; Kralja Tomislava 15; adult/child 40/20KN; 10am-6pm Tue-Fri, to 2pm Sat & Sun)

Grgur Ninski statue
STATUE

3 MAP P134, G3

Sculpted by Ivan Meštrović, this gargantuan statue is one of the defining images of Split. Its subject, a 10th-century Croatian bishop, fought for the right to use old Croatian in liturgical services instead of Latin. Notice that his left big toe has been polished to a shine – it's said that rubbing the toe brings good luck and guarantees that you'll come back to Split. (Kralja Tomislava bb)

Our-Lady-of-Health Church
CHURCH

4 MAP P134, D1

Completed in 1937, this striking Modernist church is notable for the simple, clean lines of its architecture. It's attached to a friary, founded in 1723 by Franciscans fleeing Turkish-ruled Bosnia. Inside, tall, square, granite-lined columns support a soaring ceiling, while a vast 1959 fresco by Ivo Dulčić fills the entire back wall. It depicts a stylised Christ rising above a multitude of peasants in folk costumes, milling about on an outline of the Adriatic Coast. (Gospa od zdravlja; 📞021-344 988; www.gospa-od-zdravlja.com; Trg Gaje Bulata 3; ⏰7am-noon & 5-8pm)

Split Ethnographic Museum
MUSEUM

5 ◉ MAP P134, G5

This mildly interesting museum occupies a former convent built within what was originally the emperor's bed chambers. Downstairs are temporary exhibitions, while elsewhere there's a collection of traditional costumes, jewellery, lace, weapons, toys and tools. Make sure you climb the reconstructed Roman staircase that leads to the Renaissance terrace encircling the top of the vestibule; the views are reason enough to visit the museum. (Etnografski muzej Split; 📞021-344 161; www. etnografski-muzej-split.hr; Iza Vestibula 4; adult/child 20/10KN; ⏰9.30am-8pm Mon-Sat, to 1pm Sun Jun-Sep, 9.30am-6pm Mon-Fri, 10am-2pm Sat & Sun Oct, 9.30am-4pm Mon-Fri, to 2pm Sat Nov-May)

Riva (waterfront promenade)

Archaeological Museum

A treasure trove of classical sculpture and mosaics is displayed at this excellent **museum** (Arheološki muzej; ☏021-329 340; www.armus. hr; Zrinsko-Frankopanska 25; adult/child 20/10KN; ☺9am-2pm & 4-8pm Mon-Sat Jun-Sep, closed Sat afternoon & Sun Oct-May), a short walk north of the town centre. Most of the vast collection originated from the ancient Roman settlements of Split and neighbouring Salona (Solin), and there's also some Greek pottery from the island of Vis. A lot of the most interesting items, including the larger statues and sarcophagi, are arranged outside in the cloister. There are displays of jewellery and coins, and a room filled with artefacts dating from the Palaeolithic to the Iron Age.

Eating

Gušt   PIZZA $

6 🍴 MAP P134, F1

Split's diehard pizza fans swear by this joint – it's cheap and very local, serving delicious pizza with Neapolitan-style chewy bases. The stone and brick walls make it a cosy retreat in winter. (☏021-486 333; www.pizzeria-gust.hr; Slavićeva 1; pizzas 40-62KN; ☺9am-11pm Mon-Sat)

Kruščić   BAKERY $

7 🍴 MAP P134, D3

Spit's best bakery serves delicious bread, pastries and pizza slices. The focus is more savoury than sweet, although you'll find sweet things, too. (☏099 26 12 345; www. facebook.com/Kruscic.Split; Obrov 6; items 6-15KN; ☺8am-2pm)

Makrovega   VEGETARIAN $

8 🍴 MAP P134, B3

Hidden away down a lane and behind a courtyard, this meat-free haven serves macrobiotic, vegetarian, vegan and some raw food. Seitan and tofu appear in pasta, curry and salads, and there are excellent cakes. It's somewhat lacking in atmosphere, though. (☏021-394 440; www.makrovega.hr; Leština 2; mains 60-75KN; ☺10am-10pm Mon-Fri, to 5pm Sat; 🛜)

Luka   SWEETS $

9 🍴 MAP P134, C1

Little Luka is as sweet as they come, serving muffins, cakes and coffee to locals on one of the inner city's least touristy squares. In summer there are queues out the door for the homemade ice cream. (Svačićeva 2; items 8-12KN; ☺8.30am-11pm Mon-Sat, 10am-11pm Sun; 🛜)

Konoba Fetivi
DALMATIAN, SEAFOOD $$

10 ❌ MAP P134, A5

Informal and family run, with a TV screening sports in the corner, Fetivi feels more like a tavern than most that bear the *konoba* name. However, that doesn't detract from the food, which is first rate. Seafood is the focus here. The cuttlefish stew with polenta is highly recommended, but the whole fish is wonderfully fresh, too. (☑021-355 152; www.facebook.com/KonobaFetivi; Tomića stine 4; mains 70-95KN; ⊙noon-11pm Tue-Sun)

Konoba Matejuška
DALMATIAN, SEAFOOD $$

11 ❌ MAP P134, A5

This cosy, rustic tavern, in an alleyway minutes from the seafront, specialises in well-prepared seafood – as epitomised in its perfectly cooked fish platter for two. The grilled squid is also excellent, served with the archetypal Dalmatian side dish, *blitva* (Swiss chard with slightly mushy potato, drenched in olive oil). Book ahead. (☑021-814 099; www.konobamatejuska.hr; Tomića Stine 3; mains 75-140KN; ⊙noon-11pm Apr-Oct, to 9pm Wed-Mon Nov-Mar)

Villa Spiza
DALMATIAN $$

12 ❌ MAP P134, F3

A locals' favourite, just outside the walls of Diocletian's Palace, this low-key joint offers daily-changing, great-quality Dalmatian mainstays – calamari, risotto, veal – at reasonable prices. The colourful interior has only one table and some bench seating, so be prepared to wait. (Kružićeva 3; mains 50-100KN; ⊙noon-midnight Mon-Sat)

Konoba Marjan
DALMATIAN, SEAFOOD $$$

13 ❌ MAP P134, A4

Offering great-quality Dalmatian fare, this friendly little Veli Varoš tavern features daily specials such as cuttlefish *brujet* (a flavour-packed seafood stew – highly recommended), *gregada* (fish stew with potato) and prawn pasta. The wine list is excellent, showcasing some local boutique wineries, and there are a few seats outside on the street leading up to Marjan Hill. (☑098 93 46 848; www.facebook.com/konobamarjan; Senjska 1; mains 84-160KN; ⊙noon-11pm Mon-Sat; 🛜)

Zoi
MEDITERRANEAN $$$

14 ❌ MAP P134, F6

Accessed by a discreet door on the waterfront promenade, this upstairs restaurant serves sophisticated modern Mediterranean dishes that look as divine as they taste. The decor is simultaneously elegant and extremely hip, with the exposed walls of Diocletian's Palace offset with bright bursts of magenta. Head up to the roof terrace for one of Split's most memorable dining spaces. (☑021-637 491; www.zoi.hr; Obala hrvatskog narodnog preporoda 23; mains 120-180KN; ⊙6.30pm-midnight)

Portofino

ITALIAN $$$

15 🍴 MAP P134, G4

Spilling onto a surprisingly quiet square at the heart of Diocletian's Palace, Portofino will charm the pants off you with its friendly service, elegant decor, complimentary *amuse-bouches* and delicious pasta dishes. Other specialities include steak and seafood. (☎091 38 97 784; www.facebook.com/portofinosplit; Poljana Grgura Ninskog 7; mains 95-250KN; ⏰5-11pm)

Zinfandel

EUROPEAN $$$

16 🍴 MAP P134, F4

The vibe might be more like that of an upmarket wine bar, but the food here is top notch, too. The menu includes delicious risotto, home-made pasta with fresh truffles, burgers, steaks and fish, and to wash it down there's a huge choice of local wine by the glass. Good beer selection, too. (☎021-355 135; www.zinfandelfoodandwinebar.com; Marulićeva 2; mains 140-270KN; ⏰8am-midnight Mon-Sat)

Brasserie on 7

MODERN EUROPEAN $$$

17 🍴 MAP P134, D5

The best of the Riva eateries; this waterfront brasserie's outdoor tables are the perfect vantage point for watching the passing parade. Start the day with a cooked breakfast, end it with a cocktail, and fill the hours in between with a light lunch, a more substantial dinner, or wine and a cheese platter. The service is excellent, too. (☎021-27 233; www.brasserieon7.com; Obala hrvatskog narodnog preporoda 7; mains breakfast 68-94KN, lunch 88-150KN, dinner 105-240KN; ⏰7.30am-11.30pm Apr-Sep, 8am-4pm Oct-Mar)

Chops.Grill

GRILL $$$

18 🍴 MAP P134, C2

Chops, steak, chicken breast, duck breast, tuna, sea bass, lobster, scampi – you name it, they'll grill it. Don't skimp on the sides; the truffle mash is delicious. Gas flames lend a flash of colour and movement to this simple, modern space. (☎091 36 50 000; www.chops-grill.com; Tončićeva 4; mains 90-250KN; ⏰8am-midnight)

Drinking

Marcvs Marvlvs Spalatensis

WINE BAR

19 🍺 MAP P134, G4

Fittingly, the 15th-century Gothic home of the 'Dante of Croatia', Marko Marulić, now houses this wonderful little 'library jazz bar' – small rooms crammed with books and frequented by ageless bohemians, tortured poets and wistful academics. Cheese, chess, cards and cigars are all on offer, and there's often live music. (www.facebook.com/marvlvs; Papalićeva 4; ⏰11am-midnight Jun-Aug, to 11pm Mon-Sat Sep-May; 🛜)

Paradox

WINE BAR

20 🚇 MAP P134, B4

This stylish wine and cheese bar has a fantastic rooftop terrace, a massive selection of Croatian wines (more than 120, including 40 by the glass) and an array of local cheeses to go with them. The clued-up staff members really know their stuff, and there's live music most weekends. (📞 021-787 778; www.paradox.hr; Bana Josipa Jelačića 3; ⏰ 8am-midnight; 📶)

D16

CAFE

21 🚇 MAP P134, G4

D16's baristas are serious about coffee and they've got the beards to prove it. Hidden away in the back lanes of Diocletian's Palace, this hip little speciality roaster is your best bet for a superbly executed flat white, cold brew or espresso with almond milk. Just be prepared to pay double the price you'd pay at a local-style cafe. (📞 091 79 00 705; www.d16coffee. com; Dominisova 16; ⏰ 7am-7pm Mon-Sat, 9am-7pm Sun; 📶)

Fabrique

BAR

22 🚇 MAP P134, B4

Big, bright and brash, this large industrial-style bar has offset its brick arches with kooky light fixtures and elegant little tables where the Splitćani glitterati hold court over beer and barbecue. Local craft beers feature heavily on the extensive list, alongside a range of speciality gins and tonics. The vibe gets clubby as the night progresses. (📞 098 17 51 271;

Vis Island (p142)

Vis Island

Of all the inhabited Croatian islands, Vis is the furthest from the coast and the most enigmatic. It spent much of its recent history serving as a Yugoslav military base, cut off from foreign visitors from the 1950s right up until 1989. This isolation preserved the island from development and drove much of the population to move elsewhere in search of work. As has happened with impoverished islands across the Mediterranean, the lack of development in Vis has become its drawcard. Travellers flock here seeking authenticity, nature, gourmet delights and peace and quiet. The 2018 release of the movie *Mamma Mia! Here We Go Again,* filmed on the island, has only increased its appeal.

A friendly rivalry exists between **Vis Town** and **Komiža**, the two main settlements. The former was historically associated with the nobility, while Komiža is proud of its working-class fishing heritage and pirate tales. Vis Town has the better restaurants, including **Pojoda** (☎021-711 575; Don Cvjetka Marasovića 10, Kut; mains 50-115KN; ☉noon-1am Mar-Oct, 6-10pm Nov-Feb; ☎), which serves local seafood specialties in a courtyard dotted with bamboo and citrus trees.

The most unspoilt beaches can be found on the southern and eastern sides of the island. Tiny **Stiniva** is Vis' most perfect cove. The high cliffs surrounding it form an almost complete circle, with a gap of only about 10m open to the sea. The beach is lined with large, smooth pebbles, which blaze white against the blue waters. Stiniva can be reached by an extremely steep and rough track, but it's much more easily accessed by boat.

Near the fishing village of Rukavac, **Srebrna** (Silver) beach has large white pebbles and clear blue waters, backed with a nature reserve. It has the advantage of being a flat walk from a parking area. Nudists head to **Bili Bok**, a rock terrace a little to the south.

While the rest of the island is rocky or pebbly, Vis' eastern end has a few sandy beaches. **Milna** sits right beside the main road, a sandy beach with strikingly blue water and several small islands forming an idyllic backdrop. However, you're better off taking a 15-minute walk along the shrub-lined path at the southern end of the beach to neighbouring **Zaglav**, which is even prettier and quieter. Sadly, both beaches tend to catch rubbish washing in from the sea.

Car ferries (per person/car 54/340KN, 2¼ hours) and high-speed catamarans (55KN, 1½ to 2½ hours, daily) head between Vis Town and Split.

www.fgroup.hr; Trg Franje Tuđmana 3; ⊙9am-2am May-Oct, to midnight Nov-Apr; 🛜)

St Riva BAR

23 🚇 MAP P134, F5

Bad techno and tacky cocktails don't stop St Riva being a great place to hang out. Grab a perch on the narrow terrace built into the walls of Diocletian's Palace and watch the mayhem on the Riva below. Later in the night, a fair bit of booty-shaking happens in the small, clubby space inside. (Obala hrvatskog narodnog preporoda 18; ⊙7am-midnight; 🛜)

Luxor CAFE

24 🚇 MAP P134, F5

Touristy, yes, but this cafe-bar is a great place to have coffee and cake right in the ceremonial heart of Diocletian's Palace. Cushions are laid out on the steps and there's live music nightly. (☏021-341 082; www.facebook.com/Lvxor1700; Peristil bb; ⊙8am-midnight; 🛜)

Fluid BAR

25 🚇 MAP P134, F5

This chic little place, with cushions on the lane, is great for a cocktail and a spot of people-watching. (☏095 67 00 002; www.facebook.com/fluid.split; Dosud 1; ⊙9am-1am Jun-Aug, 6pm-1am Fri & Sat Sep-May)

Galerija CAFE, BAR

26 🚇 MAP P134, G4

Locals come here to catch up with friends without loud music drowning out the conversation – except during the weekend DJ sessions. Plus it stocks soy milk – a rarity in these parts. The interior is cosy and elegant, with printed cushions, interesting art, chandeliers and a velveteen couch. In summer the action spills out onto a tiny square. (Vuškovićeva 3; ⊙8am-midnight Mon-Sat, 10am-midnight Sun)

Academia Ghetto Club BAR, CLUB

27 🚇 MAP P134, E5

Split's most bohemian bar has ancient Roman walls, a large courtyard with a trickling fountain, a chandelier-bedecked piano lounge and a small red-walled club space with poetry on the walls. The music is great, but the service can be shockingly bad. (☏099 67 18 308; Dosud 10; ⊙4pm-midnight; 🛜)

Teak CAFE, BAR

28 🚇 MAP P134, F3

Teak's terrace and antique-style interior is super popular for coffee and chats during the day, and harder drinks in the evenings. (Majstora Jurja 11; ⊙8am-midnight Mon-Sat, 10am-2pm & 7pm-midnight Sun; 🛜)

Kaštela

If you're looking to hunker down in safety, you can't do much better than having the mountains behind you and the sea in front. At least that's what the Dalmatian nobility thought when faced with the threat of Ottoman invasion in the 15th and 16th centuries. One after the other, rich families from Split headed to the 20km stretch of coast between Trogir and Split to build their sturdy mansions, until a total of 17 castles and towers were built, some with fortified villages attached. The Turks never reached them and many of the castles remain today.

Kaštela is now a municipality in its own right, incorporating seven separate towns, each named after a castle, which together form the second-largest settlement in Split-Dalmatia County. The main highway heads through its industrial fringes, leaving a less-than-positive impression, but turn off towards the water and a different Kaštela comes into view.

Kaštel Sućurac has an appealing strip of waterfront cafes and a historic core set around the ruins of a Gothic-style 15th-century bishop's palace. The bell tower is all that remains of a 16th-century church, which was destroyed in an Allied bombing raid in 1943.

At the centre of the **Kaštel Gomilica** waterfront is **Kaštilac**, a square-shaped fortified island linked to the mainland by a bridge. It was built for a community of Benedictine nuns and is now filled with private dwellings. *Game of Thrones* fans will recognise it as one of the locations used for the town of Braavos.

Kaštel Lukšić is home to the largest and best preserved of Kaštela's castles. Built in the late 15th and early 16th centuries, Dvorac Vitturi was home to the Vitturi family right up until 1943, when it was converted into a school. Now it's a small **museum** (Muzej grada Kaštela; ☏ 021-260 245; www.muzej-grada-kastela.hr; Lušiško Brce 1; adult/child 15/5KN; ⊙ 9am-8pm Mon-Fri, 6-9pm Sat, 9am-1pm Sun Jun-Sep, 9am-4pm Mon-Fri, to 1pm Sat Oct-May), with one of the upstairs rooms devoted to archaeology (containing Roman coins, jewellery and pottery) and another to the lifestyles of the local nobility (with displays of furniture, weapons and clothing).

Bus 37 heads between Split and Trogir every 20 minutes and stops in all the Kaštela towns. Kaštela is best explored on foot or by bike, as the streets are narrow, parking is terrible and the road signage isn't great.

Entertainment

Croatian National Theatre Split
THEATRE

29 ⭐ MAP P134, D1

Theatre, opera, ballet and concerts are presented at this gorgeous theatre, built in 1891. Tickets can be bought at the box office or on-line. (Hrvatsko narodno kazalište Split; 📞021-306 908; www.hnk-split.hr; Trg Gaje Bulata 1)

Split City Puppet Theatre
THEATRE

30 ⭐ MAP P134, C3

Although shows are mainly in Croatian, there's a fair chance your toddlers can speak fluent puppet. (Gradsko kazalište lutaka Split; 📞021-395 958; www.gkl-split.hr; Tončićeva 1)

Kinoteka Zlatna Vrata
CINEMA

31 ⭐ MAP P134, G4

Classic films, art flicks and retrospectives are screened at this university-affiliated cinema. It has few screenings during July and August. (📞021-361 524; www.zlatnavrata.hr; Dioklecijanova 7)

Kino Karaman
CINEMA

32 ⭐ MAP P134, C4

Mainstream cinema serving up local releases and Hollywood movies with subtitles. (📞021-348 676; www.ekran.hr; Ilićev prolaz bb)

Shopping

Arterija
FASHION & ACCESSORIES

33 🔒 MAP P134, F4

A showcase for local designer Gorana Gulišija (and a curated selection of the work of others from the region), this little store stocks interesting women's clothes, jewellery and shoes. (📞091 54 77 141; Vuškovićeva 5; 🕐10am-9pm May-Oct, 10am-2pm & 4-8pm Mon-Fri, 10am-2pm Sat Nov-Apr)

Bag & Co
FASHION & ACCESSORIES

34 🔒 MAP P134, G3

Call into this little shop to check out Ana Gjivoje's range of bright and patterned handbags, tote bags and shoulder bags, many of which

Croatian National Theatre Split

LEONID ANDRONOV/SHUTTERSTOCK ©

Local Buses

Promet Split (📞021-407 888; www.promet-split.hr) operates local buses on an extensive network throughout Split (per journey 11KN) and as far afield as Klis (13KN), Solin (13KN), Kaštela (17KN), Trogir (17KN) and Omiš (22KN). You can buy tickets on the bus, but if you buy from the local bus station or from a kiosk, a two-journey (ie return, known as a 'duplo') central-zone ticket costs only 17KN. Buses run about every 15 minutes from 5.30am to 11.30pm.

are made from recycled materials. (📞091 51 43 126; www.bagbyag.com; Majstora Jurja 17; ⏰9am-9pm Apr-Nov)

Think Pink   FASHION & ACCESSORIES

35 📍 MAP P134, D4

Boho women's clothing and jewellery made by home-grown designers. There's a second **store** (Marulićeva 1; ⏰9am-9pm) around the corner. (Zadarska 4; ⏰9am-9pm)

Studio Naranča   DESIGN

36 📍 MAP P134, G3

Showcasing the work of local artist Pavo Majić, 'Studio Orange' sells original art and very cool T-shirts, tote bags and postcards featuring his designs. (📞021-344 118; www.

studionaranca.com; Majstora Jurja 5; ⏰10am-7pm Mon-Sat, to 2pm Sun May-Sep)

Uje   FOOD & DRINKS

37 📍 MAP P134, E4

For a little place, Uje stocks a large range of top-quality Croatian olive oil, along with locally made jam, pasta sauce, *rakija* (grappa), wine, soap and wooden products. (📞021-342 719; www.uje.hr; Marulićeva 1; ⏰8am-8.30pm Mon-Fri, to 2pm Sat)

Fish Market   MARKET

38 📍 MAP P134, D4

As stinky and chaotic a scene as you could possibly imagine, Split's indoor-outdoor fish market is a spectacle to behold. Locals head here on a daily basis to haggle for all their scaly and slimy requirements from their favourite chain-smoking vendors. It's all over by about 11am, bar the dregs. (Ribarnica; Obrov 5; ⏰6.30am-2pm)

Diocletian's Cellars   MARKET

39 📍 MAP P134, F6

The main passage through the basement of Diocletian's Palace is lined with stalls selling jewellery, gifts made from Brač stone, scarves, T-shirts, handmade soap and prints. For a touristy souvenir strip, the quality's actually pretty good. (Obala hrvatskog narodnog preporoda bb; ⏰9am-9pm)

Green Market MARKET

40 🔒 MAP P134, H6

This open-air market is the place to come to stock up on fruit, vegetables and cut flowers. While it's busiest in the mornings, a few stallholders stay open to sell cherries and strawberries to tourists throughout the afternoon in summer. (Hrvojeva bb; ⊘6.30am-2pm)

Old Market MARKET

41 🔒 MAP P134, H5

Split's main outdoor market spreads throughout the streets immediately east of Diocletian's Palace. Unlike at the neighbouring Green Market, the bulk of the stalls sell durable goods such as clothes, beach towels, snorkelling masks, Croatian football shirts and a fair bit of tourist tat. (Stari Pazar)

Croatia Records MUSIC

42 🔒 MAP P134, E3

It seems that the revival of vinyl isn't limited to Western hipsters. This little store carries a selection of both LPs and CDs, featuring local and international artists. (☎021-346 494; www.crorec.hr; Narodni trg 11; ⊘8am-8pm Mon-Fri, 9am-4pm Sat)

Pickled sardines at Split's Fish Market

Worth a Trip 👀
Salona

The ruins of the ancient city of Salona, situated at the foot of the mountains northeast of Split, are of huge archaeological significance. It's a vast, sprawling site, part of which is covered by farmland and the modern-day town of Solin. Yet enough ruins remain to make this a must-see for Roman-history buffs and an interesting excursion for everyone else.

📞 021-213 358

Don Frane Bulića bb, Solin

adult/child 30/15KN

🕙 9am-7pm Mon-Sat, to 2pm Sun

Manastirine & Tusculum

Various sarcophagi are scattered about the area known as **Manastirine**, at the northern edge of the site. Positioned outside the ancient walls, this was a burial place for early Christian martyrs. In the 4th century a church was built above the tomb of St Domnius, but this was destroyed during a barbarian attack. The substantial foundations and truncated columns standing today are what remains of the major 5th-century basilica that replaced it. After the fall of Salona, the saint's remains were eventually transferred to Split Cathedral.

The most recent burial here was that of Salona's ground-breaking archaeologist Monsignor Frane Bulić (1846–1934). In 1898 he was responsible for building **Tusculum** nearby, as a base for his research. It's here that you can pay the site's admission charge and peruse displays on the site's early archaeological digs in the house's Roman-style drawing room. Most of the numerous treasures unearthed at Salona are now on display in Split's excellent Archaeological Museum (p138).

Episcopal Centre & Public Baths

From Tusculum, a path bordered by cypresses runs south to the northern city wall. This section of wall was built around 170 AD to enclose a new settlement that had sprung up east of the original walls, doubling the size of the walled city.

From here you can get an overview of the foundations of buildings that compose the **Episcopal Centre**, including a three-aisled 5th-century cathedral with an octagonal baptistery, and the remains of Bishop Honorius' basilica, built in the form of a Greek cross. The ruins of public **baths** (thermae) sit just across the narrow lane at the rear of the basilica.

★ **Top Tips**

⊙ You can access Salona's ruins from several points, including any of the lanes on the Solin side. There's no fence; people live among the ruins.

⊙ The admission charge seems rather arbitrary and it's rarely enforced, unless you actually step into the Tusculum museum or arrive on a tour bus.

✕ **Take a Break**

There are several eateries in neighbouring Solin, none of which is exceptional. The best is probably **Konoba Girasole** (☏ 021-262 215; Kralja Zvonimira 4; mains 40-130KN; ⊙ 8am-midnight), a reasonably priced, family-style tavern.

★ **Getting There**

Split city bus 1 (single/return 13/22KN) stops outside the Salona parking lot every half-hour, departing from Trg Gaje Bulata.

Porta Caesarea

Just beyond the Episcopal Centre is the **Porta Caesarea**, a monumental gate built in the 1st century as the main entrance to the original city. After the walls were extended it marked the transition between the old and new halves of Salona.

Grooves in the stone road left by ancient wheels can still be seen here, along with the remains of a covered aqueduct that ran along the top of the wall, supplying Salona with water from the Jadro River.

Five Martyrs Basilica, Amphitheatre & Forum

The main path through the city's older half follows the line of the northern wall. Just to the right of the path (ie outside the wall) is a row of 16 sarcophagi that were uncovered in 1871, all of which had been damaged and looted during the fall of Salona.

A little further on are the ruins of the **Five Martyrs Basilica** (Kapljuč basilica), built over the graves of a Christian priest and four praetorian guards who were killed for their beliefs in the nearby amphitheatre in 304.

Salona's huge **amphitheatre** was built into the northwestern corner of the city walls in the 2nd century. The building remained substantially intact until the 17th century, when the Venetians destroyed it in order to prevent it from being used as a refuge for the invading Turks. Now only the lower part of the walls remains standing, just enough to give a good impression of the layout

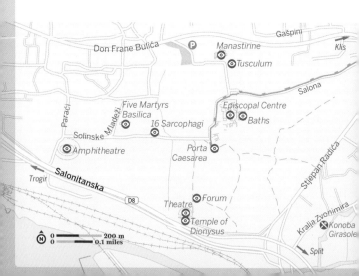

Salona: Genesis to Apocalypse

Salona was first mentioned as an Illyrian town in 119 BC and it's thought that it already had walls by then. The Romans seized the site in 78 BC and under the rule of Augustus it became the administrative headquarters of the empire's Dalmatian province.

Roman rule eventually brought peace and prosperity to the region, and Salona gained all the cultural accoutrements of Roman life, such as temples, baths and an amphitheatre. The Romans built a series of roads reaching to the Aegean and Black Seas and the Danube, facilitating trade and the expansion of Roman culture. The roads also accelerated the later spread of Christianity.

Diocletian was born near Salona around AD 244 and distinguished himself as a military commander before becoming emperor in 285. As ruler, Diocletian attempted to simplify the unwieldy empire by dividing it into two administrative halves. In 305 he retired to the grand seaside palace he had built for himself near Salona, which is estimated to have had a population of around 60,000 people at the time.

Christianity reached this region in its very earliest days. In the Bible, St Paul talks of preaching in Illyricum in his letter to the Romans (written in about AD 56), while his second letter to Timothy mentions St Titus preaching in Dalmatia. In 313, only two years after Diocletian's death, the Emperor Constantine decriminalised Christianity, and in 380 it became the only tolerated religion under Theodosius the Great.

Theodosius was the last Roman leader to rule a united empire. On his death in AD 395, the empire was divided into eastern and western realms. The Western Empire fell in 476, following invasions by various barbarian' tribes. The Goths took control of Dalmatia until 535, when the Byzantine (Eastern Roman) Emperor Justinian booted them out.

In the 7th century, Salona was levelled by the invading Avars and then the Slavs. The inhabitants fled to take refuge within Diocletian's old palace walls and on the neighbouring islands, leaving the city to decay.

At one time it could accommodate 18,000 spectators, which conveys an idea of the size and importance of ancient Salona.

Further ruins can be found among the vineyards and orchards to the left of the main path, including the scant remains of the **Forum** and, nearby, the rather more substantial ruins of a 3000-seat **theatre**. Wedged between the theatre and the busy highway is a small **Temple of Dionysus**.

Worth a Trip 🔭
Klis Fortress

Controlling the top of the valley leading into Split from the mountains, this imposing fortress spreads along a limestone bluff, reaching 385m at its highest point. Its long and narrow form (304m by 53m) derives from constant extensions over the course of millennia. For fans of Game of Thrones, Klis Fortress is Meereen – the city where Daenerys Targaryen had all those nasty slave-masters crucified in season four.

Tvrđava Klis
📞 021-240 578
www.tvrdavaklis.com
Klis bb
adult/child 40/15KN
🕓 9.30am-4pm

Walls & Gates

There are three gates to pass through before you reach the inner part of the fortress. The ticket office is located in the main gate at the lower end of the complex, built by the Austrians in the 1820s. From here a path twists up to the second gate, which was the main entrance in the Middle Ages – although its current form is also courtesy of the Austrians. The last gate, also medieval, is reached by a set of stone steps at the far end of the fort. Its current appearance is from a Venetian reconstruction in 1763.

Historical Displays

A series of highly informative but very wordy panels detailing Klis' long and complicated history is displayed in a 17th-century, Venetian-built armoury in the inner part of the fortress. In a nutshell it goes like this: founded by the Illyrians in the 2nd century BC; taken by the Romans; became a stronghold of medieval Croatian duke Trpimir; resisted attacks for 25 years before falling to the Turks in 1537; briefly retaken in 1596 before returning to Turkish control; finally fell to the Venetians in 1648. The room also contains a collection of 17th- to 19th-century muskets, swords and armour, and a mock-up of the sort of garb worn by the Uskoks, the local warriors who defended the castle against the Turks.

Upper Fortress

The views from the entire fortress are remarkable, but no less so than at the very top, taking in all of Split and the islands beyond. If you're having trouble visualising Klis in its *Game of Thrones* guise, there's a display of stills from the show in an 18th-century gunpowder chamber. At the heart of the upper fortress is a simple, square church topped with a dome, dedicated to St Vitus (Sv Vid). During the Turkish occupation it was converted into a mosque.

★ **Top Tips**

○ In summer, time your visit for the morning. It gets scorching hot up there and there's little shade.

○ If you've hired a car for the day, Klis can easily be combined with a trip to the ruins of Salona.

✕ **Take a Break**

Klis is famous for its spit-roasted lamb restaurants, and Split residents have been heading to **Restoran Perlica** (☎ 021-240 004; www.restoran-perlica.hr; Trg Grlo 1; mains 50-150KN; ⊙ 9am-10pm; 🅿 🛜 👶) for a meaty, fatty, smoky, garlicky fix since 1877. To get here from the fortress, continue along the main road for 1.7km (about 20 minutes on foot).

★ **Getting There**

Klis is located 12km northeast of Split's city centre, and can be reached by city bus 22 (13KN) from Trg Gaje Bulata or Split's local bus station.

Worth a Trip 🔭
Trogir

Gorgeous Trogir (called Trau by the Venetians) is set within medieval walls on a tiny island, linked by bridges to both the mainland and to the far larger Čiovo Island. On summer nights everyone gravitates to the wide seaside promenade, lined with bars, cafes and yachts, leaving the knotted, maze-like marble streets gleaming mysteriously under old-fashioned streetlights.

Bus Split city bus 37 takes the coastal road every 20 minutes; faster intercity buses use the highway.

Boat In summer a small boat shuttles between Trogir and Split.

Town Gate & Museum

Trogir's main **gate** (Gradska vrata) faces the bridge to the mainland, topped by a statue of the Blessed Ivan Orsini, Trogir's first bishop. The old town has retained many intact and beautiful buildings from its age of glory between the 13th and 15th centuries. In 1997 its profuse collection of Romanesque and Renaissance buildings earned it World Heritage status. As you enter through the gate, the building directly ahead is the former Garagnin-Fanfogna palace, now home to a **museum** (Muzej grada Trogira; ☏ 021-881 406; www.muzejgradatrogira.blogspot.com; Gradska vrata 4; adult/child 20/15KN; ⊙10am-1pm & 6-9pm daily Jul & Aug, Mon-Sat Jun & Sep, 9am-2pm Mon-Fri Oct-May) exhibiting books, documents, drawings and period costumes from the city's long history.

St Lawrence's Cathedral

Trogir's showstopping attraction is its triple-naved **cathedral** (Katedrala svetog Lovre; ☏ 021-881 426; Trg Ivana Pavla II; 25KN; ⊙8am-8pm Mon-Sat, noon-6pm Sun Jun-Aug, to 6pm Sep-May), one of the finest architectural works in Croatia, built between the 13th and 15th centuries. The grand Romanesque **portal**, flanked by a nude Adam and Eve standing on the backs of lions, was carved by Master Radovan in 1240. At the end of the portico is another fine piece of sculpture: the 1464 cherub-filled **baptistery** sculpted by Andrija Aleši.

Inside, don't miss the richly decorated 15th-century **Chapel of Blessed Ivan Orsini**, halfway along the left-hand wall. Be sure to take a look at the **treasury**, which contains an ivory triptych and various silver reliquaries. You can also climb the 47m-high cathedral **bell tower** for views over the old town.

★ **Top Tips**

○ While it's easily reached on a day trip from Split, Trogir also makes a good alternative base to the big city and a relaxing place to spend a few days.

✕ **Take a Break**

Rustic **Konoba Trs** (☏ 021-796 956; www.konoba-trs. com; Matije Gupca 14; mains 105-230KN; ⊙11am-midnight Mon-Sat, 5pm-midnight Sun) has wooden benches and old stone walls inside, and an inviting courtyard shaded by grapevines. The menu adds clever, contemporary twists to Dalmatian classics.

Trg Ivana Pavla II

Abutting the cathedral, 'John Paul II Square' is lined with many of Trogir's most outstanding buildings. The **Grand Cipiko Palace** (Velika palača Cipiko; Gradska 41), directly opposite the cathedral, was home to a prominent family during the 15th century. It's not open to the public, but you can stop to admire the intricately carved Gothic triforium encasing the windows on the facade, the work of Andrija Aleši.

Across the square, the open-sided, 13th-century **Town Loggia** contains an interesting relief by famous 20th-century Croatian sculptor Ivan Meštrović. Next to it is **St Sebastian's Church**, built in 1476 and topped by a large, blue-faced Renaissance clock. Inside are stone sarcophagi and the photos of locals killed in the 1990s war.

Next up is the **Sacred Art Museum** (Muzej sakralne umjetnosti; ☎021-881 426; Trg Ivana Pavla II 6; 10KN; ◷8am-8pm Mon-Sat, 11.30am-7pm Sun Jun-Sep). Highlights include illuminated manuscripts, a large painting of *St Jerome and St John the Baptist* by Bellini, an almost life-size, brightly painted *Crucifix with Triumphant Christ* and the darkly lit fragments of a 13th-century icon that once adorned the cathedral's altar.

Adjacent is the 15th-century **Town Hall** (Gradska vijećnica; Trg Ivana Pavla II 1; ◷7am-7pm Mon-Fri) which has a Gothic courtyard decorated with coats of arms, a monumental staircase and a well carved with the winged lion of St Mark, the symbol of the Venetian Republic. It houses the **tourist office** (☎021-885 628;

Trogir's Origins

Backed by high hills in the north, surrounded by water on all sides and snug within its walls, Trogir proved an attractive place to settlers. It was founded in the 3rd century BC by Greek colonists and later became Romanised. Its defensive position allowed Trogir to maintain a degree of autonomy throughout Croatian and Byzantine rule, while trade and nearby mines ensured its economic viability.

In the 13th century sculpture and architecture flourished, reflecting a vibrant, dynamic culture. When Venice bought Dalmatia in 1409, Trogir refused to accept the new ruler and the Venetians bombarded the town into submission. While the rest of Dalmatia stagnated under Venetian rule, Trogir continued to produce great artists who enhanced the beauty of the town.

www.tztrogir.hr; Trg Ivana Pavla II 1; ☺8am-8pm May-Sep, 9am-5pm Mon-Fri Oct-Apr).

St Nicholas's Convent

The treasury of this Benedictine **convent** (Samostan svetog Nikole; ☏02-881 631; Gradska 2; adult/child 10/5KN; ☺10am-1pm & 4.15-5.45pm Jun-Sep, by appointment other times) is home to a dazzling 3rd-century relief of Kairos, the Greek god of opportunity, carved out of orange-hued marble.

Small Loggia

This historic open-sided **market** (Mala loža; Obala Bana Berislavića 11; ☺9am-9pm May-Sep), pressed up against the town walls, is still used by street traders, although these days they mainly deal in jewellery. It's a good place to buy interesting pieces showcasing local stone and pearls.

Kamerlengo Castle

Built by the Venetians in around 1420, this **fortress** (Kaštel Kamerlengo; Hrvatskog proljeća 1971 bb; adult/child 25/20KN; ☺9am-7pm) was once connected to the city walls. Inside it's basically an empty shell, but you can climb up and circle the walls. Concerts are held here in July and August during the Trogir Summer Festival; posters advertising the events are displayed all around town.

Marmont's Gloriette

This elegant gazebo was built by the French during the Napoleonic occupation of Dalmatia. At the time it jutted out into a marshy lagoon and Marshal Marmont, governor-general of the French empire's Illyrian Provinces, used to sit within the circle of columns, surrounded by water, and play cards.

Survival Guide

Dubrovnik (p33) CHALFFY/GETTY IMAGES ©

Before You Go

Book Your Stay

○ Dalmatia is well set up for tourism, with accommodation to suit every price point – although in the height of summer you won't find many bargains and you'll need to book well in advance.

○ Dubrovnik has a great accommodation selection ranging from hostels to luxurious hotels, but it's the most expensive place to stay in Croatia at every price point. Nearby Cavtat is a cheaper alternative.

○ Split and Hvar Town have competitive hostel scenes, but private rooms edge out of the budget range in summer.

○ There are affordable private rentals available throughout the region.

Best Budget

Hostel Angelina (www. hostelangelinaoldtown dubrovnik.com) Cute Dubrovnik hostel with bunks, guest kitchen and bougainvillea-

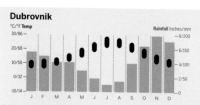

When to Go

High Season (Jun–Aug) The warmest weather and a full roster of festivities but overflowing with tourists. Prices at their highest.

Shoulder (Apr, May, Sep & Oct) Sunny, less crowded, and usually warm enough for swimming.

Low Season (Nov–Apr) Cold and wet, prices are low, ferry schedules are reduced, many places close.

shaded terrace views.

Hostel Marina Trogir (www.hostelmarina -trogir.com) Excellent hostel with custom-built wooden bunks with suitcase-sized lockers underneath, reading lights and privacy curtains.

Vintage Hostel Makarska (www.hostelmak arska.com) Long-time favourite with a brand new extension.

Villa Ana (www.villa -ana-bol.com) Friendly, family-managed apartments on the eastern fringes of Bol.

Pansion Ivan & Ivana (www.pansionivanand

ivana.com) Three spacious bedrooms and a self-contained apartment, in Bol.

Best Midrange

Korta (www.kortasplit. com) Simple but elegant apartments in Split's historic Veli Varoš neighbourhood.

Villa Luka's (www. villalukas.com) Modern block in Cavtat, with 12 attractive apartments and a small pool.

Apartments Magdalena (www.magdalena -apartments.com) Three comfortable, well-equipped apartments in Split.

Karmen Apartments
(www.karmendu.com)
Four inviting apart-
ments, a stone's throw
from Dubrovnik's old
harbour.

**Korčula Royal Apart-
ments** (www.korcula
royalapartments.com)
Smartly furnished
apartments in an old
stone villa, just outside
the old town.

Best Top End

**Heritage Hotel
Antique Split** (www.
antique-split.com)
Palace living at its most
palatial.

**MirÓ Studio Apart-
ments** (www.mirostudio
apartmentsdubrovnik.
com) Schmick apart-
ments on the edge of
Dubrovnik's old town.

Villa Split (www.
villasplitluxury.com)
Boutique B&B built into
the wall of Diocletian's
Palace.

Maritimo (www.hotel
-maritimo.hr) Midsize
hotel, right by the beach
in Makarska.

Hotel Božica (www.
hotel-bozica.hr) Mod-
ern 30-room hotel on
the quiet Elafiti Island
of Šipan.

Arriving in Dalmatia

Dubrovnik Airport

Dubrovnik Airport
(DBV, Zračna luka Du-
brovnik; ☏ 020-773 100;
www.airport-dubrovnik.
hr) In Čilipi, 19km
southeast of Dubrovnik.
Croatia Airlines, British
Airways, Iberica, Turk-
ish Airlines and Vueling
fly to Dubrovnik all
year round. In summer
they're joined by dozens
of other airlines flying
seasonal routes and
charter flights.

Airport Shuttle Bus
(☏ 020-642 286; www.
atlas-croatia.com; one way/
return 40/70KN) Timed
around flight schedules.
Buses to Dubrovnik stop
at the Pile Gate and the
bus station; buses to the
airport pick up from the
bus station and from
the bus stop near the
cable car.

**City buses 11, 27 and
38** Stop at the airport
but are less frequent
and take longer (28KN,
seven daily, no Sunday
service).

Taxi Allow up to 280KN
for a taxi to Dubrovnik.
Dubrovnik Transfer Ser-
vices (www.dubrovnik
-transfer-services.
com) offers a set-price
taxi transfer to the city
(€30) and Cavtat (€16).

Split Airport

Split Airport (Zračna
luka Split, SPU; Map p74;
A1; ☏ 021-203 555; www.
split-airport.hr; Dr Franje
Tuđmana 1270, Kaštel
Štafilić) Located 24km
northwest of central
Split, in Kaštela. In
summer, dozens of
airlines fly here from all
over Europe (including
Austrian Airlines, Brit-
ish Airways, easyJet,
Norwegian Air Shuttle
and Scandinavian Air-
lines). Croatia Airlines,
Eurowings and Trade
Air operate year round.

Airport Shuttle Bus
(☏ 021-203 119; www.
plesoprijevoz.hr; one
way 30KN) Makes the
30-minute journey
between the airport and
Split's main bus station
(platform 1) at least 14
times a day.

City buses 37 & 38
The regular Split–Trogir
bus stops near the air-
port every 20 minutes.
The journey takes 50

minutes from the local bus station on Domovinskog Rata, making it a slower but cheaper option than the shuttle (17KN from Split, 13KN from Trogir).

Taxi A cab to central Split costs between 250KN and 300KN.

Brač Airport

Brač Airport (BWK; Map p74, B2; ☎ 021-559 711; www.airport-brac.hr) Located 14km northeast of Bol and 38km southeast of Supetar. It only has scheduled commercial flights mid-May to September. Destinations include Zagreb, Ljubljana, Bern, Luxembourg, Brussels and Rotterdam. No public transport from the airport, so you'll need to take a taxi, which costs about 150KN to Bol (300KN to Supetar).

Getting Around

Air

○ Croatia Airlines has flights between Dubrovnik and Split from May to October.

Boat

○ Numerous ferries connect Split, Dubrovnik and their surrounding islands year-round, with services extended in the tourist season.

○ Locals use the term 'ferry' to refer exclusively to car ferries and 'catamaran' to refer to the faster, passenger-only ferry services.

○ **Jadrolinija** (☎ 021-338 333; www.jadrolinija.hr) is the main operator, with **Kapetan Luka** (Krilo; ☎ 021-645 476; www.krilo.hr) and **G&V Line** (☎ 020-313 119; www.gv-line.hr; Obala Ivana Pavla II 1, Gruž) also offering catamaran services.

○ Boats are comfortable and well equipped; most offer free wi-fi.

○ Outside of the busiest times, it's usually possible to simply turn up and buy your ticket from a kiosk at the wharf.

○ In most instances you can buy tickets online, although it's not always possible on the day of travel. Pre-booking doesn't guarantee you a space on a particular sailing, so it still pays to get to the wharf early in peak season, especially if you're travelling with a car.

○ Bicycles can be transported on car ferries (but not catamarans) for an additional fee (13KN to 45KN).

○ Travelling as a foot passenger gives you more flexibility and is considerably cheaper than travelling with a vehicle. In most cases you can hire a car, scooter or bicycle at your destination, should you need one.

Bus

○ Bus services are excellent and relatively inexpensive.

○ Dubrovnik (www.libertasdubrovnik.hr) and Split (www.promet-split.hr) have efficient local bus networks; a ride is usually 10KN to 15KN, with a small discount if you buy tickets at a *tisak* (newsstand).

○ Different companies handle the intercity routes, so prices can vary substantially. Enquire at the bus station or check www.vollo.net or www.getbybus.com.

○ Luggage stowed in the baggage compartment under the bus costs extra (around 10KN a piece).

o Note that buses between Split and Dubrovnik pass through Bosnian territory so you'll need to keep your passport handy.

Car & Motorcyle

o The main motorway from Zagreb to Dalmatia passes near Split but falls short of Dubrovnik by 110km. Collect a ticket from the automated booths when you enter the motorway and present it at the booths when you leave the motorway, where it's used to calculate the applicable toll.

o Car hire is available in all major towns, airports and tourist locations. Independent local companies are often much cheaper than the international chains, but the big companies offer one-way rentals.

o Third-party public liability insurance is included by law with car rentals.

o In Croatia you drive on the right, and the use of seatbelts is mandatory.

o Unless otherwise posted, the speed limits for cars and motorcycles are as follows: 50km/h in built-up areas; 90

km/h on other roads; 110km/h on main highways; 130km/h on motorways.

o It's illegal to drive with a blood-alcohol content higher than 0.05%.

o From October to March you are required to drive with your headlights on, even during the day.

o All foreign cars must have their nationality sticker on the back.

Essential Information

Accessible Travel

o Mobility-impaired travellers will find the cobbled streets and endless steps of Dalmatia's old towns challenging. Most sights aren't well set up for wheelchair users, and specific resources for sight-impaired and hearing-impaired travellers are rare. For further information, contact the **Croatian Association for the Physically Disabled** (Hrvatski savez udruga tjelesnih invalida; ☎01-48 12 004; www.hsuti.hr).

o Public toilets at bus stations, train stations, airports and large public venues are usually wheelchair-accessible. Large hotels are wheelchair-accessible, but very little private accommodation is.

o Bus and train stations in Split and Dubrovnik are wheelchair-accessible, but the ferries are not.

Business Hours

Opening hours vary throughout the year. We've provided high-season opening hours; hours generally decrease in the shoulder and low seasons.

Banks 8am or 9am to 8pm weekdays and 7am to 1pm or 8am to 2pm Saturday.

Cafes and bars 8am or 9am to midnight.

Offices 8am to 4pm or 8.30am to 4.30pm weekdays.

Post offices 7am to 8pm weekdays and 7am to 1pm Saturday; longer hours in coastal towns in summer.

Restaurants Noon to 11pm or midnight; often closed Sundays outside peak season.

Shops 8am to 8pm weekdays, to 2pm or 3pm Saturday; some take a 2pm to 5pm break. Shopping malls have longer hours.

Discount Cards

o If you want to get through all the essential sights of Dubrovnik in one day, it's worth buying the Dubrovnik Card (190KN). If you were already planning on walking the city walls (admission 150KN) and buying a museum pass (120KN), it makes a lot of sense. It also scores you free rides on buses and discounts at various restaurants and shops. It can be purchased online at a discounted rate (www.dubrovnikcard. com), or at tourist offices, travel agencies, hotels and museums.

o Split's tourist offices stock the free 72-hour Split Card, which offers free or discounted access to attractions, car rental, restaurants, shops and theatres. You're eligible for the card if you're staying in Split more than four nights from April to September, or staying

in designated hotels for more than two nights at other times.

Dos & Don'ts

Greetings Friends and family, both male and female, greet each other with a kiss on each cheek – never a single kiss. If you go in for a third kiss (as they do in Serbia), a Croatian will even it up with a fourth – it can never be an odd number. Don't panic – if locals are greeting a tourist, a handshake is more usual.

Dining out If you head out for a drink or meal with a Croat, whoever does the inviting should do the paying. It's an unspoken rule that the other person should even the score next time around.

Dining in If you're lucky enough to be invited to a local's house for dinner, come with an empty stomach (force-feeding is a national obsession) and a small gift such as chocolates or flowers. If you bring flowers, there must always be an uneven number of stems.

Electricity

Type F
230V/50Hz

LGBTIQ+ Travellers

o Homosexuality is generally tolerated if not widely accepted and public signs of same-sex affection may be met with hostility.

o There are no specifically gay or lesbian venues in Dalmatia, but there is a popular gay beach on Lokrum island.

o Split Pride (www.face book.com/lgbt.pride. split) is usually held on the first Saturday in June.

Money

o Croatia uses the kuna (KN). Each kuna is divided into 100 lipa.

○ Many accommodation providers set their prices in euros. It's often possible to pay in euro notes, but credit-card charges are invariably billed in kuna.

○ ATMs can be found throughout Dalmatia and are tied in with international networks such as Cirrus and Maestro.

○ Visa and MasterCard are widely accepted in hotels but rarely accepted in any kind of private accommodation. Diners Club and American Express are less accepted and many smaller restaurants and shops do not take any credit cards at all.

○ Tipping is purely discretionary and is generally only done in restaurants (up to 10%) and cafebars (round up to the nearest round figure).

Public Holidays

Croats take their holidays very seriously. Shops and museums are shut and boat services are reduced. On religious holidays, the churches are full; it can be a good time to check out the artwork in a church that is usually closed.

New Year's Day
1 January

Epiphany 6 January

Easter Sunday & Monday March/April

Labour Day 1 May

Corpus Christi 60 days after Easter

Day of Antifascist Resistance 22 June

Statehood Day 25 June

Homeland Thanksgiving Day 5 August

Feast of the Assumption 15 August

Independence Day 8 October

All Saints' Day 1 November

Christmas 25 & 26 December

Tourist Information

Bol (☏ 021-635 638; www.bol.hr; Porat Bolskih Pomoraca bb; ⊙ 8.30am-10pm Jul & Aug, 8.30am-2pm & 4-8pm Jun & Sep, 8.30am-2pm & 4-8pm Mon-Sat May & Oct, 8.30am-2pm Mon-Fri Nov-Apr)

Dubrovnik (☏ 020-312 011; www.tzdubrovnik.hr; Brsalje 5; ⊙ 8am-8pm)

Hvar Town (☏ 021-741 059; www.tzhvar.hr; Trg Sv Stjepana 42; ⊙ 8am-10pm Jul & Aug, 8am-8pm Mon-Sat, 8am-1pm & 4-8pm Sun Jun & Sep, 8am-2pm Mon-Fri, to noon Sat Oct-May)

Korčula Town (☏ 020-715 701; www.visitkorcula.eu; Obala dr Franje Tuđmana 4; ⊙ 8am-8pm Jun-Aug, 8am-3pm Mon-Sat May, Sep & Oct, 8am-2pm Mon-Fri Nov-Apr)

Makarska (☏ 021-612 002; www.makarska-info.hr; Obala kralja Tomislava 16; ⊙ 8am-8pm)

Split: Peristil (☏ 021-345 606; www.visitsplit.com; Peristil bb; ⊙ 8am-9pm Jun-Sep, 8am-8pm Mon-Sat, to 5pm Sun Apr, May & Oct, 9am-4pm Mon-Fri, to 2pm Sat Nov-Mar),

Split: Riva (☏ 021-360 066; www.visitsplit.com; Obala hrvatskog narodnog preporoda 9; ⊙ 8am-9pm Jun-Sep, 8am-8pm Mon-Sat, to 5pm Sun Apr, May & Oct, 9am-4pm Mon-Fri, to 2pm Sat Nov-Mar)

Visas

Citizens of many countries can stay visa-free for up to 90 days within a 180-day period. Check on the website of the Croatian Ministry for Foreign & European Affairs (www.mvep.hr).

Language

Croatian pronunciation is not difficult – in the Croatian writing system every letter is pronounced and its sound does not vary from word to word. The sounds are pretty close to their English counterparts. Note that in our pronunciation guides *zh* is pronounced as the 's' in 'pleasure'. The stressed syllable is indicated with italics in our pronunciation guides.

To enhance your trip with a phrasebook, visit lonelyplanet. com. Lonely Planet iPhone phrasebooks are available through the Apple App store.

Basics

Hello.
Bok.   bok

Goodbye.
Zbogom.   *zbo*·gom

Yes./No
Da./Ne.   da/ne

Please.
Molim.   *mo*·leem

Thank you.
Hvala.   *hva*·la

Excuse me.
Oprostite.   o·*pro*·stee·te

Sorry.
Žao mi je.   *zha*·o mee ye

My name is ...
Zovem se ...   *zo*·vem se ...

What's your name?
Kako se zovete/   *ka*·ko se *zo*·ve·te/
zoveš?   *zo*·vesh (pol/inf)

Do you speak (English)?
Govorite/   go·vo·*ree*·te/
Govoriš   go·vo·reesh
li (engleski)?   lee (*en*·gle·skee)
                         (pol/inf)

I (don't) understand.
Ja (ne)   ya (ne)
razumijem.   ra·*zoo*·mee·yem

Eating & Drinking

What would you recommend?
Što biste nam   shto *bee*·ste nam
preporučili?   pre·po·*roo*·
                         chee·lee

What's in that dish?
Od čega se   od *che*·ga se
sastoji ovo jelo?   *sa*·sto·yee o·vo
                         ye·lo

Please bring the bill/check.
Molim vas   *mo*·leem vas
donesite račun.   do·*ne*·see·te
                         ra·choon

Vegetarian meal.
Vegetarijanski   ve·ge·ta·*ree*·yan·
obrok.   skee o·brok

menu	*jelovnik*	ye·*lov*·neek
breakfast	*doručak*	do·roo·chak
lunch	*ručak*	roo·chak
dinner	*večera*	ve·*che*·ra
beer	*pivo*	*pee*·vo
coffee	*kava*	*ka*·va
water	*voda*	*vo*·da
tea	*čaj*	chai
with/ without	*sa/bez*	sa/bez

Shopping

I'd like to buy ...
Želim kupiti ...   zhe·leem
kupiti ...   koo·pee·tee ...

I'm just looking.
Ja samo   ya sa·mo
razgledam.   raz·gle·dam

May I look at it?
Mogu li to   mo·goo lee to
pogledati?   po·gle·da·tee

How much is it?
Koliko stoji?   ko·lee·ko sto·yee

Emergencies

Help!
Upomoć!   oo·po·moch

I'm lost.
Izgubio/   eez·goo·bee·o/
Izgubila sam se.   eez·goo·bee·la
  sam se (m/f)

Leave me alone!
Ostavite me na miru!   o·sta·vee·te
  me na mee·roo

There's been an accident!
Desila se nezgoda!   de·see·la se
  nez·go·da

Call the police!
Zovite policiju!   zo·vee·te
  po·lee·tsee·yoo

I'm ill.
Ja sam bolestan/   ya sam
bolesna.   bo·le·stan/
  bo·le·sna (m/f)

Time & Numbers

What time is it?
Koliko je sati?   ko·lee·ko ye sa·tee

It's (10) o'clock.
(Deset) je sati.   (de·set) ye sa·tee

Half past (10).
(Deset) i po.   (de·set) ee po

morning   *jutro*   yoo·tro

evening   *večer*   ve·cher

yesterday	*jučer*	yoo·cher
today	*danas*	da·nas
tomorrow	*sutra*	soo·tra
1	*jedan*	ye·dan
2	*dva*	dva
3	*tri*	tree
4	*četiri*	che·tee·ree
5	*pet*	pet
6	*šest*	shest
7	*sedam*	se·dam
8	*osam*	o·sam
9	*devet*	de·vet
10	*deset*	de·set
100	*sto*	sto

Transport & Directions

left	*lijevo*	lee·ye·vo
right	*desno*	de·sno
behind	*iza*	ee·za
in front of	*ispred*	ees·pred

Where is ...?
Gdje je ...?   gdye ye ...

What's the address?
Koja je adresa?   ko·ya ye a·dre·sa

I want to go to ...
Želim da idem u ...   zhe·leem da
  ee·dem oo ...

Does it stop at (Split)?
Da li staje u   da lee sta·ye oo
(Splitu)?   (splee·too)

What time does it leave?
U koliko sati kreće?   oo ko·lee·ko
  sa·tee kre·che

What time does it get to (Zagreb)?
U koliko sati stiže   oo ko·lee·ko
u (Zagreb)?   sa·tee stee·zhe
  oo (zag·reb)

Behind the Scenes

Send Us Your Feedback

We love to hear from travellers – your comments help make our books better. We read every word, and we guarantee that your feedback goes straight to the authors. Visit **lonelyplanet.com/contact** to submit your updates and suggestions.

Note: We may edit, reproduce and incorporate your comments in Lonely Planet products such as guidebooks, websites and digital products, so let us know if you don't want your comments reproduced or your name acknowledged. For a copy of our privacy policy visit lonelyplanet.com/privacy.

Peter's Thanks

First and foremost, I'd like to say a huge hvala to Vojko, Marija, Ivan, Mario and Ivana Dragičević in Split, for the kindness and patience you've shown your distant cousin over the years. Many thanks to my Destination Editor, Anna Tyler, and all of the in-house Lonely Planet crew who have contributed to this book.

Acknowledgements

Cover photograph: Town harbour, Dubrovnik; Jordan Banks/AWL © Photographs pp 28–9 (clockwise from left): Anna Lurye/Shutterstock, cge2010/Shutterstock, xbrchx/500px ©

This Book

This 1st edition of Lonely Planet's *Pocket Dubrovnik & the Dalmatian Coast* was curated, researched and written by Peter Dragicevich. This guidebook was produced by the following:

Destination Editor
Anna Tyler

Senior Product Editor
Elizabeth Jones

Product Editor
Kate James

Senior Cartographer
Anthony Phelan

Book Designer
Ania Bartoszek

Assisting Editors Sarah Bailey, Janice Bird, Gabrielle Innes, Monique Perrin

Cover Researcher
Naomi Parker

Thanks to Vesna Čelebić, Grace Dobell

Index

See also separate subindexes for:

⊗ **Eating p172**

⊙ **Drinking p173**

✪ **Entertainment p173**

⊙ **Shopping p173**

LONELY PLANET IN THE WILD

Send your 'Lonely Planet in the Wild' photos to social@lonelyplanet.com
We share the best on our Facebook page every week!

Our Writers

Peter Dragicevich

After a successful career in niche newspaper and magazine publishing, both in his native New Zealand and in Australia, Peter finally gave into Kiwi wanderlust, giving up staff jobs to chase his diverse roots around Europe. Over the last decade he's written literally dozens of guidebooks for Lonely Planet on an oddly disparate collection of countries, all of which he's come to love. He once again calls Auckland, New Zealand his home – although his current nomadic existence means he's often elsewhere.

Published by Lonely Planet Global Limited
CRN 554153
1st edition – Apr 2019
ISBN 978 1 78868 019 6
© Lonely Planet 2019   Photographs © as indicated 2019
10 9 8 7 6 5 4 3 2 1
Printed in Malaysia

Although the authors and Lonely Planet have taken all reasonable care in preparing this book, we make no warranty about the accuracy or completeness of its content and, to the maximum extent permitted, disclaim all liability arising from its use.

All rights reserved. No part of this publication may be copied, stored in a retrieval system, or transmitted in any form by any means, electronic, mechanical, recording or otherwise, except brief extracts for the purpose of review, and no part of this publication may be sold or hired, without the written permission of the publisher. Lonely Planet and the Lonely Planet logo are trademarks of Lonely Planet and are registered in the US Patent and Trademark Office and in other countries. Lonely Planet does not allow its name or logo to be appropriated by commercial establishments, such as retailers, restaurants or hotels. Please let us know of any misuses: lonelyplanet.com/ip.